NATIVE SON

Richard Wright

TECHNICAL DIRECTOR Maxwell Krohn
EDITORIAL DIRECTOR Justin Kestler
MANAGING EDITOR Ben Florman

SERIES EDITORS Boomie Aglietti, Justin Kestler
PRODUCTION Christian Lorentzen

WRITERS Selena Ward, Dave Purcell
EDITORS Dennis Quinio, Matt Blanchard

This edition published by Spark Publishing

Spark Publishing
A Division of SparkNotes LLC
120 Fifth Avenue, 8th Floor
New York, NY 10011

Please submit all comments and questions or report errors to
www.sparknotes.com/errors.

Library of Congress information available upon request

Printed in China

ISBN 1-58663-450-X

Introduction: Stopping to Buy Sparknotes on a Snowy Evening

Whose words these are you *think* you know.
Your paper's due tomorrow, though;
We're glad to see you stopping here
To get some help before you go.

Lost your course? You'll find it here.
Face tests and essays without fear.
Between the words, good grades at stake:
Get great results throughout the year.

Once school bells caused your heart to quake
As teachers circled each mistake.
Use SparkNotes and no longer weep,
Ace every single test you take.

Yes, books are lovely, dark, and deep,
But only what you grasp you keep,
With hours to go before you sleep,
With hours to go before you sleep.

Contents

NOTE: This SparkNote refers to the 1991 Library of America edition of *Native Son*. Other editions, particularly those published before 1991, vary in a number of passages because the novel's first editors demanded that Wright tone down the sexual language of his work. The Library of America edition is based on Wright's original version.

CONTEXT

RICHARD WRIGHT WAS BORN ON SEPTEMBER 4, 1908, on a farm in Mississippi. He was the first of two sons born to Nathan Wright, an illiterate sharecropper, and Ella Wilson Wright, a schoolteacher. When Wright was a small child, his father abandoned the family to live with another woman. Wright's mother subsequently became chronically ill, and the family was forced to live with various relatives. During one particularly tumultuous period, Wright and his brother spent a month in an orphanage. The family eventually settled with Wright's grandmother. Though Wright attended a Seventh-Day Adventist school where his aunt taught, he rebelled against religious discipline, much like the character of Bigger Thomas in *Native Son.*

The illnesses suffered by Wright's mother drained the family financially, forcing Wright to work a number of jobs during his childhood and adolescence. Despite sporadic schooling, he became an avid reader and graduated as valedictorian of his junior high school. Financial troubles worsened, however, and Wright was forced to drop out of high school after only a few weeks to find work. Shortly before the beginning of the Great Depression, the family moved to Chicago, where Wright devoted himself seriously to writing.

In 1934, Wright became a member of the Communist Party and began publishing articles and poetry in numerous left-wing publications. Still his family's sole financial support, Wright took a job with the Federal Writers' Project helping research the history of blacks in Chicago. In 1937, he moved to New York, where he was Harlem editor for the *Daily Worker,* a communist newspaper. Around this time, he wrote and published *Uncle Tom's Children,* a collection of short stories that addresses the social realities faced by American black men. The novel—like its namesake, Harriet Beecher Stowe's *Uncle Tom's Cabin*—was banned or censored in parts of the United States.

However, it was Wright's 1940 novel, *Native Son,* that stirred up real controversy by shocking the sensibilities of both black and white America. The reaction to *Uncle Tom's Children* had disappointed Wright—though he had worked hard to describe racism as he saw it, he still felt he had written a novel "which even bankers' daughters could read and feel good about." With his next work, *Native Son,* he was determined to make his readers feel the reality of race relations by writing something "so hard and deep that they would have to face it without the consolation of tears." The protagonist of the novel, Bigger Thomas, hails from the lowest rung of society, and Wright does not infuse him with any of the romantic aspects or traits common to literary heroes. Rather, given the social conditions in which he must live, Bigger is what one might expect him to be—sullen, frightened, violent, hateful, and resentful.

In his essay "How Bigger Was Born," Wright explains that Bigger is a fusion of men he had himself known while growing up in the South. Confronted by racism and oppression and left with very few options in their lives, these men displayed increasingly antisocial and violent behavior, and were, in effect, disasters waiting to happen. In Chicago, removed from the terrible oppression of the South, Wright discovered that Bigger was not exclusively a black phenomenon. Wright saw, just as Bigger does in *Native Son* that millions of whites suffered as well, and he believed that the direct cause of this suffering was the structure of American society itself. *Native Son* thus represents Wright's urgent warning that if American social and economic realities did not change, the oppressed masses would soon rise up in fury against those in power.

Disenchanted over the Communist Party's attempts to control the content of his writing, Wright quietly split with the Party in 1942. He continued to be active in left-wing politics, however, and was the subject of intense FBI scrutiny throughout his life. In the late 1940s, Wright moved to Paris with his wife and daughter. He became deeply interested in the philosophical movement of existentialism, often socializing with Jean-Paul Sartre and Simone de Beauvoir, two of the movement's leading figures.

Though Wright continued writing, his career never again reached the heights it attained when *Native Son* and *Black Boy*—his popular autobiographical novel—were published in the early and mid-1940s. Wright died of a heart attack in 1960. Today he is honored as one of the finest writers in African-American literature, a tremendous influence on such eminent contemporaries and followers as Ralph Ellison, James Baldwin, and Toni Morrison, among many others.

PLOT OVERVIEW

BIGGER THOMAS, a poor, uneducated, twenty-year-old black man in 1930s Chicago, wakes up one morning in his family's cramped apartment on the South Side of the city. He sees a huge rat scamper across the room, which he corners and kills with a skillet. Having grown up under the climate of harsh racial prejudice in 1930s America, Bigger is burdened with a powerful conviction that he has no control over his life and that he cannot aspire to anything other than menial, low-wage labor. His mother pesters him to take a job with a rich white man named Mr. Dalton, but Bigger instead chooses to meet up with his friends to plan the robbery of a white man's store.

Anger, fear, and frustration define Bigger's daily existence, as he is forced to hide behind a façade of toughness or risk succumbing to despair. While Bigger and his gang have robbed many black-owned businesses, they have never attempted to rob a white man. Bigger sees whites not as individuals, but as a natural, oppressive force—a great looming "whiteness" pressing down upon him. Bigger's fear of confronting this force overwhelms him, but rather than admit his fear, he violently attacks a member of his gang to sabotage the robbery. Left with no other options, Bigger takes a job as a chauffeur for the Daltons.

Coincidentally, Mr. Dalton is also Bigger's landlord, as he owns a controlling share of the company that manages the apartment building where Bigger's family lives. Mr. Dalton and other wealthy real estate barons are effectively robbing the poor, black tenants on Chicago's South Side—they refuse to allow blacks to rent apartments in predominantly white neighborhoods, thus leading to overpopulation and artificially high rents in the predominantly black South Side. Mr. Dalton sees himself as a benevolent philanthropist, however, as he donates money to black schools and offers jobs to "poor, timid black boys" like Bigger. However, Mr. Dalton practices this token philanthropy mainly to alleviate his guilty conscience for exploiting poor blacks.

Mary, Mr. Dalton's daughter, frightens and angers Bigger by ignoring the social taboos that govern the relations between white women and black men. On his first day of work, Bigger drives Mary to meet her communist boyfriend, Jan. Eager to prove their progressive ideals and racial tolerance, Mary and Jan force Bigger to take them to a restaurant in the South Side. Despite Bigger's embarrassment, they order drinks, and as the evening passes, all three of them get drunk. Bigger then drives around the city while Mary and Jan make out in the back seat. Afterward, Mary is too drunk to make it to her bedroom on her own, so Bigger helps her up the stairs. Drunk and aroused by his unprecedented proximity to a young white woman, Bigger begins to kiss Mary.

Just as Bigger places Mary on her bed, Mary's blind mother, Mrs. Dalton, enters the bedroom. Though Mrs. Dalton cannot see him, her ghostlike presence terrifies him. Bigger worries that Mary, in her drunken condition, will reveal his presence. He covers her face with a pillow and accidentally smothers her to death. Unaware that Mary has been killed, Mrs. Dalton prays over her daughter and returns to bed. Bigger tries to conceal his crime by burning Mary's body in the Daltons' furnace. He decides to try to use the Daltons' prejudice against communists to frame Jan for Mary's disappearance. Bigger believes that the Daltons will assume Jan is dangerous and that he may have kidnapped their daughter for political purposes. Additionally, Bigger takes advantage of the Daltons' racial prejudices to avoid suspicion, continuing to play the role of a timid, ignorant black servant who would be unable to commit such an act.

Mary's murder gives Bigger a sense of power and identity he has never known. Bigger's girlfriend, Bessie, makes an offhand comment that inspires him to try to collect ransom money from the Daltons. They know only that Mary has vanished, not that she is dead. Bigger writes a ransom letter, playing upon the Daltons' hatred of communists by signing his name "Red." He then bullies Bessie to take part in the ransom scheme. However, Mary's bones are found in the furnace, and Bigger flees with Bessie to an empty building. Bigger rapes Bessie and, frightened that she will give him away, bludgeons her to death with a brick after she falls asleep.

Bigger eludes the massive manhunt for as long as he can, but he is eventually captured after a dramatic shoot-out. The press and the public determine his guilt and his punishment before his trial even begins. The furious populace assumes that he raped Mary before killing her and burned her body to hide the evidence of the rape. Moreover, the white authorities and the white mob use Bigger's crime as an excuse to terrorize the entire South Side .

Jan visits Bigger in jail. He says that he understands how he terrified, angered, and shamed Bigger through his violation of the social taboos that govern tense race relations. Jan enlists his friend, Boris A. Max, to defend Bigger free of charge. Jan and Max speak with Bigger as a human being, and Bigger begins to see whites as individuals and himself as their equal.

Max tries to save Bigger from the death penalty, arguing that while his client is responsible for his crime, it is vital to recognize that he is a product of his environment. Part of the blame for Bigger's crimes belongs to the fearful, hopeless existence that he has experienced in a racist society since birth. Max warns that there will be more men like Bigger if America does not put an end to the vicious cycle of hatred and vengeance. Despite Max's arguments, Bigger is sentenced to death.

Bigger is not a traditional hero by any means. However, Wright forces us to enter into Bigger's mind and to understand the devastating effects of the social conditions in which he was raised. Bigger was not born a violent criminal. He is a "native son": a product of American culture and the violence and racism that suffuse it.

CHARACTER LIST

Bigger Thomas The protagonist of *Native Son*. A poor, uneducated black man, Bigger comes from the lowest rung on the American social and economic ladder. As his lack of education has left him no option other than menial labor, he has felt trapped his whole life, resenting, hating, and fearing the whites who define the narrow confines of his existence. Bigger views white people as a collective, overwhelming force that tells him where to live, where to work, and what to do.

Mary Dalton The daughter of Mr. and Mrs. Dalton, Bigger's wealthy employers. Mary identifies herself as a progressive, dates an admitted communist, and interacts with Bigger with little regard for the strict boundary society imposes between black men and white women. Mary's transgression of this boundary leads to her death and the resulting development of Bigger's character.

Mr. and Mrs. Dalton A white millionaire couple living in Chicago. Mrs. Dalton is blind; Mr. Dalton has earned a fortune in real estate. Although he profits from charging high rents to poor black tenants—including Bigger's family—on Chicago's South Side, he nonetheless claims to be a generous philanthropist and supporter of black Americans.

Jan Erlone A member of the Communist Party and Mary Dalton's boyfriend—a relationship that upsets Mary's parents. Jan, like Mary, wants to treat Bigger as an equal, but such untraditional behavior only frightens and angers Bigger. Jan later recognizes his mistake in trying to treat Bigger this way and becomes sympathetic toward his plight. Jan becomes especially aware of the social divisions that prevent Bigger from relating normally with white society.

Boris A. Max A Jewish lawyer who works for the Labor Defenders, an organization affiliated with the Communist Party. Max argues, based on a sociological analysis of American society, that institutionalized racism and prejudice—not inherent ethnic qualities—create conditions for violence in urban ghettos.

Bessie Mears Bigger's girlfriend. Their relationship remains quite distant and is largely based upon mutual convenience rather than romantic love.

Mrs. Thomas Bigger's devoutly religious mother. Mrs. Thomas has accepted her precarious, impoverished position in life and warns Bigger at the beginning of the novel that he will meet a bad end if he fails to change his ways.

Buddy Thomas Bigger's younger brother. Buddy, unlike his brother, does not rebel against his low position on the social ladder. In fact, he envies Bigger's job as a chauffeur for a rich white family. As the novel progresses, however, Buddy begins to take on a more antagonistic attitude toward racial prejudice.

Vera Thomas Bigger's younger sister. Vera, like Bigger, lives her life in constant fear.

G. H., Gus, and Jack Bigger's friends, who often plan and execute robberies together. G. H., Gus, and Jack hatch a tentative plan to rob a white shopkeeper, Mr. Blum, but they are afraid of the consequences if they should be caught robbing a white man. At the beginning of the novel, Bigger taunts his friends about their fear, even though he is just as terrified himself.

Mr. Blum A white man who owns a delicatessen on the South Side of Chicago. Mr. Blum represents an inviting robbery target for Bigger and his friends, but their fear of the consequences of robbing a white man initially prevents them from following through on their plan.

Britten   A racist, anticommunist private investigator who helps Mr. Dalton investigate Mary's disappearance.

Buckley   The incumbent State's Attorney who is running for reelection. Buckley is viciously racist and anticommunist.

Peggy   An Irish immigrant who has worked as the Daltons' cook for years. Peggy considers the Daltons to be marvelous benefactors to black Americans. Though she is actively kind to Bigger, she is also extremely patronizing.

Doc   The black owner of a pool hall on the South Side of Chicago that serves as a hangout for Bigger and his friends.

Reverend Hammond The pastor of Mrs. Thomas's church who urges Bigger to turn toward religion in times of trouble.

ANALYSIS OF MAJOR CHARACTERS

BIGGER THOMAS

As the protagonist and main character of *Native Son,* Bigger is the focus of the novel and the embodiment of its main theme—the effect of racism on the psychological state of its black victims. As a twenty-year-old black man cramped in a South Side apartment with his family, Bigger has lived a life defined by the fear and anger he feels toward whites for as long as he can remember. Bigger is limited by the fact that he has only completed the eighth grade, and by the racist real estate practices that force him to live in poverty. Furthermore, he is subjected to endless bombardment from a popular culture that portrays whites as sophisticated and blacks as either subservient or savage. Indeed, racism has severely curtailed Bigger's prospects in life and even his very conception of himself. He is ashamed of his family's poverty and afraid of the whites who control his life—feelings he works hard to keep hidden, even from himself. When these feelings overwhelm him, he reacts with violence. Bigger commits crimes with his friends—though only against other blacks, as the group is too frightened to rob a white man—but his own violence is often directed at these friends as well.

Bigger feels little guilt after he accidentally kills Mary. In fact, he feels for the first time as though his life actually has meaning. Mary's murder makes him believe that he has the power to assert himself against whites. Wright goes out of his way to emphasize that Bigger is not a conventional hero, as his brutality and capacity for violence are extremely disturbing, especially in graphic scenes such as the one in which he decapitates Mary's corpse in order to stuff it into the furnace. Wright does not present Bigger as a hero to admire, but as a frightening and upsetting figure created by racism. Indeed, Wright's point is that Bigger becomes a brutal killer precisely because the dominant white culture fears that he will become a brutal killer. By confirming whites' fears, Bigger contributes to the cycle of racism in America. Only after he meets Max and learns to talk through his problems does Bigger begin to redeem himself, recognizing whites as individuals for the first time and realizing the extent to which he has been stunted by racism. Bigger's progress is cut short, however, by his execution.

Critics of *Native Son* are divided over the effectiveness of Bigger as a character. Though many have found him a powerful and disturbing symbol of black rage, others, including the eminent writer James Baldwin, have considered him too narrow to represent the full scope of black experience in America. One area of fascination has been Bigger's name, which seems to combine the words "big" and "nigger," suggesting the aggressive racial stereotype he comes to embody. As Max indicates, however, Bigger does not have a great deal of choice. The title of the novel implies that Bigger's descent into criminality and violence is an inherently American story. Bigger is not alien to or outside of American culture—on the contrary, he is a "native son."

MARY DALTON

Mary's importance to the novel stems not only from her death, which represents the clear turning point in Bigger's life, but from her insidious form of racism, which is among Wright's subtlest criticisms of white psychology. Mary self-consciously identifies herself as a progressive: she defies her parents by dating a communist, cares about social issues, and is politically and personally interested in improving the lives of blacks in America. Though Mary's intentions are essentially good, however, she is too young and immature either to commit fully to her chosen causes or to attain a sophisticated understanding of those people she seeks to help.

Mary attempts to treat Bigger as a human being, but gives no thought to the fact that Bigger might be surprised and confused by such unprecedented treatment from the wealthy white daughter of his employer. Mary simply assumes that Bigger will embrace her friendship, as she supports the political cause that she believes he represents. She does not even think to wonder about any of his personal qualities, thoughts, or feelings, but merely seeks to befriend him automatically, because he is black. For a tragically brief moment, Mary seems to recognize Bigger's discomfort, a sign that perhaps one day she could be capable of greater understanding. Ultimately, however, Mary never gets the chance to perceive Bigger as an individual.

Though Mary has the best of intentions, she treats Bigger with a thoughtless racism that is just as destructive as the more overt hypocrisy of her parents. Interacting with the Daltons, Bigger at least knows where he stands. Mary's behavior, however, is disorienting and upsetting to him. Ultimately, Mary's thoughtlessness actually ends up placing Bigger in serious danger, while the only risk she herself runs is mild punishment or disapproval from her parents for her disobedience. She does not stop to think that Bigger could easily lose his job—or worse—if he upsets her parents. Mary unthinkingly puts Bigger in the position of being alone with her in her bedroom, and her inability to understand him and the terror he feels at the prospect of being discovered in her room proves fatal.

BORIS A. MAX

The lawyer who defends Bigger at his trial, Max is a member of the Labor Defenders, a legal organization affiliated with the Communist Party. While it would seem natural for Max himself to be a communist, his party affiliation is never made explicitly clear in the novel. Max is certainly sympathetic to the communist cause, but, unlike Jan, never identifies himself as a member of the Party.

Of all the white characters in the novel, Max is able to see and understand Bigger most clearly. He speaks to Bigger as a human being, rather than simply as a black man or a murderer, which gives Bigger the chance to tell his own story for the first time in his life. Max's recognition of Bigger's humanity allows Bigger to understand for the first time that a sympathetic relationship between a white man and a black man is possible. Still, Max is unable to avoid viewing Bigger as a symbol of racial oppression—one of millions of black men just like him—and therefore is never able to understand him fully.

Critics have argued that Max is never fully defined as a character and is simply a spokesman for Wright. It is clear that Max does, in some respects, serve as a mouthpiece for the novel's sociological analysis of Bigger's condition. Though Bigger feels what is happening to him throughout the novel, he is often unable, sometimes intentionally, to grasp it consciously. Max, in his courtroom speech, is able to articulate many of these unexpressed perceptions that Bigger has felt. Max does not argue Bigger's innocence: his impassioned speech is a plea for the court to recognize Bigger for who he is and to understand the conditions that have created him. In this regard, Max serves as a voice for Wright's warning to America about the consequences of continued racial oppression.

Themes, Motifs & Symbols

Themes

Themes are the fundamental and often universal ideas explored in a literary work.

The Effect of Racism on the Oppressed

Wright's exploration of Bigger's psychological corruption gives us a new perspective on the oppressive effect racism had on the black population in 1930s America. Bigger's psychological damage results from the constant barrage of racist propaganda and racial oppression he faces while growing up. The movies he sees depict whites as wealthy sophisticates and blacks as jungle savages. He and his family live in cramped and squalid conditions, enduring socially enforced poverty and having little opportunity for education. Bigger's resulting attitude toward whites is a volatile combination of powerful anger and powerful fear. He conceives of "whiteness" as an overpowering and hostile force that is set against him in life. Just as whites fail to conceive of Bigger as an individual, he does not really distinguish between individual whites—to him, they are all the same, frightening and untrustworthy. As a result of his hatred and fear, Bigger's accidental killing of Mary Dalton does not fill him with guilt. Instead, he feels an odd jubilation because, for the first time, he has asserted his own individuality against the white forces that have conspired to destroy it.

Throughout the novel, Wright illustrates the ways in which white racism forces blacks into a pressured—and therefore dangerous—state of mind. Blacks are beset with the hardship of economic oppression and forced to act subserviently before their oppressors, while the media consistently portrays them as animalistic brutes. Given such conditions, as Max argues, it becomes inevitable that blacks such as Bigger will react with violence and hatred. However, Wright emphasizes the vicious double-edged effect of racism: though Bigger's violence stems from racial hatred, it only increases the racism in American society, as it confirms racist whites' basic fears about blacks. In Wright's portrayal, whites effectively transform blacks into their own negative stereotypes of "blackness." Only when Bigger meets Max and begins to perceive whites as individuals does Wright offer any hope for a means of breaking this circle of racism. Only when sympathetic understanding exists between blacks and whites will they be able to perceive each other as individuals, not merely as stereotypes.

THE EFFECT OF RACISM ON THE OPPRESSOR

The deleterious effect of racism extends to the white population, in that it prevents whites from realizing the true humanity inherent in groups that they oppress. Indeed, one of the great strengths of *Native Son* as a chronicle of the effects of oppression is Wright's extraordinary ability to explore the psychology not only of the oppressed but of the oppressors as well. Wright illustrates that racism is destructive to both groups, though for very different reasons. Many whites in the novel, such as Britten and Peggy, fall victim to the obvious pitfall of racism among whites: the unthinking sense of superiority that deceives them into seeing blacks as less than human. Wright shows that this sense of superiority is a weakness, as Bigger is able to manipulate it in his cover-up of Mary's murder. Bigger realizes that a man with Britten's prejudices would never believe a black man could be capable of what Bigger has done. Indeed, for a time, Bigger manages to escape suspicion.

Other white characters in the novel—particularly those with a self-consciously progressive attitude toward race relations—are affected by racism in subtler and more complex ways. Though the Daltons, for instance, have made a fortune out of exploiting blacks, they aggressively present themselves as philanthropists committed to the black American cause. We sense that they maintain this pretense in an effort to avoid confronting their guilt, and we realize that they may even be unaware of their own deep-seated racial prejudices. Mary and Jan represent an even subtler form of racism, as they consciously seek to befriend blacks and treat them as equals, but ultimately fail to understand them as individuals. This failure has disastrous results. Mary and Jan's simple assumption that Bigger will welcome their friendship deludes them into overlooking the possibility that he will react with suspicion and fear—a natural reaction considering that Bigger has never experienced such friendly treatment from whites. In this regard, Mary and Jan are deceived by their failure to recognize Bigger's individuality just as much as an overt racist such as Britten is deceived by a failure to recognize Bigger's humanity. Ultimately, Wright portrays the vicious circle of racism from the white perspective as well as from the black one, emphasizing that even well-meaning whites exhibit prejudices that feed into the same black behavior that confirms the racist whites' sense of superiority.

The Hypocrisy of Justice

An important idea that emerges from Wright's treatment of racism is the terrible inequity of the American criminal justice system of Wright's time. Drawing inspiration from actual court cases of the 1930s—especially the 1938–39 case of Robert Nixon, a young black man charged with murdering a white woman during a robbery—Wright portrays the American judiciary as an ineffectual pawn caught between the lurid interests of the media and the driving ambition of politicians. The outcome of Bigger's case is decided before it ever goes to court: in the vicious cycle of racism, a black man who kills a white woman is guilty regardless of the factual circumstances of the killing.

It is important, of course, that Bigger is indeed guilty of Mary's murder, as well as Bessie's. Nonetheless, the justice system still fails him, as he receives neither a fair trial nor an opportunity to defend himself. With the newspapers presenting him as a murderous animal and Buckley using the case to further his own political career, anything said in Bigger's defense falls on deaf ears. Even Max's impassioned defense is largely a wasted effort. The motto of the American justice system is "equal justice under law," but Wright depicts a judiciary so undermined by racial prejudice and corruption that the concept of equality holds little meaning.

Motifs

Motifs are recurring structures, contrasts, or literary devices that can help to develop and inform the text's major themes.

Popular Culture

Throughout *Native Son,* Wright depicts popular culture—as conveyed through films, magazines, and newspapers—as a major force in American racism, constantly bombarding citizens with images and ideas that reinforce the nation's oppressive racial hierarchy. In films such as the one Bigger attends in Book One, whites are depicted as glamorous, attractive, and cultured, while blacks are portrayed as jungle savages or servants. Wright emphasizes that this portrayal is not unique to the film Bigger sees, but is replicated in nearly every film and every magazine. Not surprisingly, then, both blacks and whites see blacks are inferior brutes—a view that has crippling effects on whites and absolutely devastating effects for blacks. Bigger is so influenced by this media saturation that, upon meeting the Daltons, he is completely unable to be himself. All he can do is act out the role of the subservient black man that he has seen in countless popular culture representations. Later, Wright portrays the media as one of the forces that leads to Bigger's execution, as the sensationalist press stirs up a furor over his case in order to sell newspapers. The attention prompts Buckley, the State's Attorney, to hurry Bigger's case along and seek the death penalty. Wright scatters images of popular culture throughout *Native Son,* constantly reminding us of the extremely influential role the media plays in hardening already destructive racial stereotypes.

RELIGION

Religion appears in *Native Son* mostly in relation to Bigger's mother and Reverend Hammond. Bigger's mother relies on her religion as a source of comfort in the face of the crushing realities of life on the South Side. Bigger, however, compares his mother's religion with Bessie's whiskey drinking—an escapist pastime with no inherent value. At times, Bigger wishes he were able to enjoy the comfort religion brings his mother, but he cannot shake his longing for a life in this world. When Reverend Hammond gives Bigger a cross to wear while he is in prison, Bigger equates the cross with the crosses that are burned during racist rituals. In making this comparison, Wright suggests that even the moral province of Christianity has been corrupted by racism in America.

COMMUNISM

Wright's portrayal of communism throughout *Native Son,* especially in the figures of Jan and Max, is one of the novel's most controversial aspects. Wright was still a member of the Communist Party at the time he wrote this novel, and many critics have argued that Max's long courtroom speech is merely an attempt on Wright's part to spread communist propaganda. While Wright uses communist characters and imagery in *Native Son* generally to evoke a positive, supportive tone for the movement, he does not depict the Party and its efforts as universally benevolent. Jan, the only character who explicitly identifies himself as a member of the Party, is almost comically blind to Bigger's feelings during Book One. Likewise, Max, who represents the Party as its lawyer, is unable to understand Bigger completely. In the end, Bigger's salvation comes not from the Communist Party, but from his own realization that he must win the battle that rages within himself before he can fight any battles in the outside world. The changes that Wright identifies must come not from social change, but from individual effort.

SYMBOLS

Symbols are objects, characters, figures, or colors used to represent abstract ideas or concepts.

MRS. DALTON'S BLINDNESS

Mrs. Dalton's blindness plays a crucial role in the circumstances of Bigger's murder of Mary, as it gives Bigger the escape route of smothering Mary to keep her from revealing his presence in her bedroom. On a symbolic level, this set of circumstances serves as a metaphor for the vicious circle of racism in American society: Mrs. Dalton's inability to see Bigger causes him to turn to violence, just as the inability of whites to see blacks as individuals causes blacks to live their lives in fear and hatred. Mrs. Dalton's blindness represents the inability of white Americans as a whole to see black Americans as anything other than the embodiment of their media-enforced stereotypes. Wright echoes Mrs. Dalton's literal blindness throughout the novel in his descriptions of other characters who are figuratively blind for one reason or another. Indeed, Bigger later realizes that, in a sense, even he has been blind, unable to see whites as individuals rather than a single oppressive mass.

THE CROSS

The Christian cross traditionally symbolizes compassion and sacrifice for a greater good, and indeed Reverend Hammond intends as much when he gives Bigger a cross while he is in jail. Bigger even begins to think of himself as Christlike, imagining that he is sacrificing himself in order to wash away the shame of being black, just as Christ died to wash away the world's sins. Later, however, after Bigger sees the image of a burning cross, he can only associate crosses with the hatred and racism that have crippled him throughout his life. As such, the cross in *Native Son* comes to symbolize the opposite of what it usually signifies in a Christian context.

SNOW

A light snow begins falling at the start of Book Two, and this snow eventually turns into a blizzard that aids in Bigger's capture. Throughout the novel, Bigger thinks of whites not as individuals, but as a looming white mountain or a great natural force pressing down upon him. The blizzard is raging as Bigger jumps from his window to escape after Mary's bones are found in the furnace. When he falls to the ground, the snow fills his mouth, ears, and eyes—all his senses are overwhelmed with a literal whiteness, representing the metaphorical "whiteness" he feels has been controlling him his whole life. Bigger tries to flee, but the snow has sealed off all avenues of escape, allowing the white police to surround and capture him.

Summary & Analysis

NOTE: Native Son *is divided into four sections: three "Books" and a chapter entitled "How Bigger Was Born." We have divided each of these sections into several parts for the purposes of summary and analysis.*

Book One (part one)

From the opening through Bigger's argument with Gus at the pool hall

Summary

An alarm clock rings in a dark Chicago apartment. Bigger Thomas, a young black man, shares the apartment with his mother, his sister Vera, and his brother Buddy. The apartment has only one room, which forces Bigger and Buddy to turn their backs to avoid the shame of seeing Vera and their mother dress.

A huge black rat runs across the floor. Vera cowers and Mrs. Thomas jumps on the bed while Bigger and Buddy frantically try to kill the rat. The rat attacks Bigger, biting a hole in his pant leg before it is cornered. Bigger smashes the rat with a skillet and then crushes its head with a shoe, cursing hysterically. Before disposing of the rat, Bigger holds it up by the tail in front of Vera, taking pleasure in her fear until she faints.

With the immediate danger gone, Mrs. Thomas turns all her attention on Bigger, first asking him why he has frightened his sister, then blaming him for the family's poverty and accusing him of thinking only of himself. She warns him that if he does not change his ways and stop associating with his "gang," he will end up in the gallows. Bigger tries to shout his mother down, but his voice is filled with nervousness and irritation, and he longs for silence.

Bigger hates his family because of their poverty and suffering and because he feels there is nothing he can do to help them. He believes that he cannot afford to let himself feel their shame and misery too strongly without also feeling the urge to kill himself or someone else. He has cultivated a façade of outer toughness to protect himself from the unbearable pressure he feels as a result of his family's social position.

Bigger's mother sings a spiritual while preparing breakfast—a song that annoys Bigger. She begins to prod Bigger about a job he has been offered with a man named Mr. Dalton. She tells him that if he takes the job, the family will be able to move to a nicer apartment. If he does not, he will lose his relief money and the family will starve. Resentment builds in Bigger, as he feels that his family is tricking him into giving up. Frustrated by his narrow range of choices, he storms out of the room and into the building's vestibule, where he broods while watching the traffic through the window.

Across the street, men are putting up campaign posters for the State's Attorney, a man named Buckley. Bigger imagines the millions of dollars Buckley makes through corruption, and longs to be him for a day. The words "If You Break The Law, You Can't Win!" adorn the top of the campaign posters. Bigger knows, however, that a man can win if he can afford to pay Buckley off. Bigger checks his pocket and finds he has only twenty-six cents.

Bigger and his friends have a tentative plan to rob a delicatessen owned by a white man named Mr. Blum. The gang has committed other robberies, but never one against a white man, partly because Bigger knows that white policemen are largely unconcerned with black-against-black crimes. Robbing a white man would mean entering new territory, "a symbolic challenge" to white rule.

Bigger's friend Gus meets him on the street and they watch an airplane write out an advertisement in white smoke. Bigger states that he could fly a plane if he were given the chance. Gus agrees that Bigger could, but only if he had some money and were not black. Bigger complains that whites will not let blacks do anything, and he feels as though he is living in prison.

Gus and Bigger playact at being white, alternately portraying a military general, the fantastically wealthy white businessman J. P. Morgan, and the president of the United States. Gus and Bigger act out a skit in which the president wants to keep the "niggers" under control. After the playacting, Bigger tells Gus he is certain that something bad is going to happen to him. Gus agrees when Bigger says that he can feel the presence of whites inside himself. Whenever he thinks of white people, he has the sensation that a fire is burning in his stomach and feels that he might do something uncontrollable and rash.

Gus and Bigger go to Doc's pool hall to meet their friends Jack and G. H. Bigger asks them to join a game for which Gus is paying, and they all laugh. Bigger laughs along, but because he is broke he worries that the joke is on him. He brings up the plan to rob Mr. Blum and accuses his friends of being too fearful to carry out the plan. Jack and G. H. agree to do the job, but Gus keeps quiet. Bigger accuses Gus of being afraid to rob a white man and hates Gus for that fear. Inside, however, Bigger feels this fear himself. Gus remains silent until Bigger snaps, shouting and swearing at Gus. Gus blames Bigger's bad temper for causing most of the gang's troubles and accuses Bigger of being afraid himself. Bigger becomes furious and threatens to hit Gus. Finally, Gus agrees to the plan to rob Blum. While Bigger struggles to control his impulse to fight Gus, the four agree to meet at Doc's at three o'clock to carry out the robbery. G. H. takes Gus away from the pool hall.

ANALYSIS

Native Son opens with the ringing bell of an alarm clock—a wake-up call not only for Bigger and his family, but also a warning to America as a whole about the dangerous state of race relations in the country in the 1930s. Wright sees a black population that, though freed from outright slavery, still lives under terrible conditions, is unable to vote, and is terrorized by groups like the Ku Klux Klan. The North is somewhat more integrated, but many blacks there still live in desperate poverty. Wright believes these conditions have created individuals who are isolated not only from the white world but also from their own religion and culture—people whose only release is through violence. Bigger is the epitome of such individual: he is alienated from his family and friends, annoyed by his mother's religious songs, and kept poor and impotent through the oppressiveness of white society.

The title of Book One is "Fear," and that fear appears in the first pages of this section with the appearance of a large black rat. The rat is just as afraid of Bigger as Bigger is of the rat, and their reactions to these fears are the same: defiance and violence. This first book might just as easily have been called "Shame," as Bigger also feels that emotion acutely. The suffering his family endures while living in such terrible conditions constantly reminds Bigger how powerless he is to help them. The knowledge of his family's situation is more than he can bear, so he attempts to keep a cold and reserved attitude toward his family and himself. Bigger's need to hide behind such a wall of toughness is one of the many ways in which we see him trapped by his circumstances. He is caught in a tiny apartment with failure, inadequacy, shame, and fear pervading his life. He has access only to menial jobs and feels he lacks any control over his existence or direction. He also feels trapped inside himself, unable to acknowledge the misery he feels without risking his own destruction. Throughout the novel, we see that when Bigger is cornered, like the rat, he is overwhelmed by shame and fear and lashes out with violence, the only weapon at his disposal.

Here, Wright begins to develop Bigger's view of whites as an overwhelming force that sweeps him toward doom. *Native Son* is written in the style of urban naturalism, much like Upton Sinclair's *The Jungle*. The characters in these works are urban residents whose fates are determined by forces almost completely beyond their control. Like the main character of *The Jungle*, a poor Lithuanian immigrant in Chicago, Bigger perceives that the narrow boundaries of his life were already determined before his birth. A long-standing unequal division of power between white and black, rich and poor has trapped him within a disadvantaged race and a disadvantaged class. He feels watched and controlled even when white people are not present, as if white people invade his very insides. He feels like a man condemned to a degraded existence and certain doom. This sense of doom is heightened by Buckley's campaign slogan: "If You Break The Law, You Can't Win!" The State's Attorney is a powerful member of the institution of white justice, and his poster foreshadows Bigger's losing battle with white authority.

BOOK ONE (PART TWO)

From the movie theater through Bigger's fight with Gus

SUMMARY

> *Was what he had heard about rich white people really true? Was he going to work for people like you saw in the movies . . . ?*
>
> (See QUOTATIONS, p. 61)

Bigger decides to spend twenty cents on a movie to help dispel his growing fear of robbing Blum. He and Jack go to a movie theater, and they masturbate while watching it and thinking about their girlfriends. Afterward, they discuss Bigger's upcoming job interview with Mr. Dalton. Bigger says that he would rather go to jail than take a job through the relief agency. A newsreel begins, showing the young daughters of wealthy families playing on the beach in Florida. The camera focuses on Mary Dalton as she kisses a handsome man, identified only as a "well-known radical." A commentator reports that Mary has shocked her family by becoming romantically linked to this man and that her parents have tried to put an end to the relationship. Bigger realizes that the scandalous young woman is the daughter of his prospective employer, Mr. Dalton.

The movie *Trader Horn* begins. Watching scenes of black men and women dancing wildly to the beat of drums, Bigger imagines a party at a rich, white home. For the first time, he contemplates the job with the Daltons with great interest. Mary Dalton, he thinks, might be a "hot kind of girl" who would like to come see his side of town, and who might bribe him to keep her secrets from her parents. Bigger also remembers his mother's constant advice that wealthy white people treat black people better than they treat poor whites. Bigger thinks that perhaps the Dalton family would be easy to get along with because they are so wealthy. His thoughts return to the robbery of Mr. Blum. Now that he is more interested in a real job, he berates himself for taking a "fool's chance" with the law.

When Jack and Bigger return to Doc's at three o'clock, Bigger is secretly glad that Gus is not there yet, as they cannot carry out the robbery without him. As the group anxiously awaits Gus, nervous tension gathers in the pit of Bigger's stomach, as he has convinced himself that he no longer wants to follow through with the robbery. When Gus finally shows up, the anxious Bigger attacks and beats him violently without provocation or warning. He then pulls a knife on Gus and forces him to lick the blade. Bigger accuses Gus of ruining the plan by being late, although Jack insists there is still enough time. Gus flees the premises, and G. H. hints that Bigger had wanted to spoil the plan all along. Bigger threatens G. H. and Doc draws a gun. Bigger slashes the cloth on the pool table before slipping out the door and heading home. Though he does not know it consciously, he feels "instinctively" that it was his fear of robbing a white man that drove him to attack Gus. Bigger's survival depends on how well he can bury this knowledge deep inside himself.

ANALYSIS

In this section, we see that popular culture serves as a release for Bigger—a way to help him forget his misery—but that it also serves as a form of indoctrination. As Bigger has limited contact with white people, his understanding of the white world comes primarily through the popular culture of movies, magazines, and hearsay. The movies focus on the gleaming, opulent world of fabulously wealthy white Americans like the Daltons. Blacks, if they appear in the movies at all, are consistently depicted as one of two stereotypes: either the dangerous, radically foreign, and inferior savage; or the clownish, humble, and ignorant black servant. The white society that produces this popular culture, then, has control over the social dialogue that determines the meaning of the color of Bigger's skin and hence his identity.

Ultimately, white America controls Bigger's relationship with his own community. He is too afraid to challenge white authority, so his own community becomes the target and outlet for his relentless terror and frustration. He has an intense desire to test the boundaries of the subservience white America has assigned him, but he is ultimately too afraid to carry out the robbery of a white merchant. Instead, he transfers his hatred and fear of whites onto his friend Gus. Gus is a safer target, just as the black merchants are safer targets for the gang's robberies. This violence against members of their own community, however, ruins blacks' chances of becoming a real community and keeps them alienated and weak.

The wall of isolation behind which Bigger hides alienates him not only from his friends, family, and community, but also from himself. His fear, rage, and conflicting and unexamined desires torture him. He instinctively understands that it is better to fight Gus than to rob a white man, but he must keep this understanding buried beneath his consciousness. There exists, then, a gulf between what Bigger feels and what he knows. Unable to face the reality of his life as a black man, Bigger is forced to keep his thoughts and his feelings separate. His consciousness is divided, just as the members of his own community are divided and unable to come together into a cohesive and productive whole.

BOOK ONE (PART THREE)

From Bigger's arrival at the Daltons' to meeting Mary with the car

SUMMARY
Bigger watches the sunset from his apartment window as he waits for his appointment with Mr. Dalton. He feels his gun inside his shirt

him. Peggy tells Bigger how nice the Daltons are and how much they do for "your people," meaning blacks. Peggy also tells Bigger that the last chauffeur, a black man named Green, was with the Daltons for ten years. Green attended night school at Mrs. Dalton's urging and went on to a government job. After Bigger finishes dinner, Peggy instructs him in the operation of the furnace, then shows him to his room. Bigger excitedly contemplates the luxuries he will enjoy with the Daltons. Nonetheless, Mary still worries him. Every rich white woman he has met in the past has treated him in a cold and reserved manner, but Mary does not. Bigger therefore does not know what to make of her.

Before driving Mary out to the university, Bigger enters the kitchen and finds Mrs. Dalton sitting there alone. She asks him several questions about his education. Bigger feels that Mrs. Dalton judges him in the same way his mother does. However, Bigger does note a difference between the manners in which the two women treat him: whereas Bigger's mother tries to impose her own desires on him, Mrs. Dalton wants him to do "the things she felt that *he* should have wanted to do." Bigger thinks to himself that he does not want to go to school. He feels he has "other plans," but he is unable to articulate them, even to himself. He pulls the Daltons' car out of the garage and picks Mary up at the side door.

ANALYSIS

In Bigger's first visit to the Daltons', we see the extreme discomfort he experiences when he is surrounded by white society. Bigger sees white people not as individuals, but rather as an undifferentiated "whiteness," a powerful, threatening, and hateful authority that denies him control over his own life and identity. The structure of American society and Bigger's own limited, restricted experiences prevent him from relating to white people in any other way. Though Bigger feels that wrong is being done to him, he has so deeply internalized the rules of race relations that he finds himself acting out the role he has always seen blacks assume around rich, powerful whites.

The Daltons demonstrate similarly conflicting racial attitudes. As a real estate baron, Mr. Dalton is a major player in the production of the "whiteness" that terrifies, oppresses, and enrages Bigger. Despite Bigger's criminal record, Mr. Dalton gives him a job because he thinks that blacks deserve a chance. Nonetheless, there is condescension in Mr. Dalton's manner and charity. He simultaneously

and considers leaving it at the apartment, but ultimately decid
bring it with him. Bigger does not fear the Daltons, but he kr
that blacks are often harassed in white neighborhoods and bel
the gun will help make him equal to the whites.

Upon arriving at the Daltons', Bigger is unsure wheth
should enter at the front or the back of the house. He stands ou
the imposing iron fence of the Daltons' mansion and is filled w
mixture of fear and hate, feeling foolish for having though
might like this job. He summons the courage to go to the front
which the Daltons' white maid, Peggy, answers. Though Peg
polite to Bigger, he senses that she is looking down on him
though she, like him, is only hired help. While Bigger waits fo
Dalton, he gawks at the splendor of the home, with its elegan
nishings and paintings. He feels intimidated by the vast differ
between this world and his own. Assailed by insecurity, ten
and fear, he becomes awkward and clumsy.

Mr. Dalton, a tall, white-haired man, appears and leads B
toward his office. Mr. Dalton is the owner of the real estate
pany that owns the building in which Bigger and his family li
a hallway, they pass Mrs. Dalton, whose face and hair are so v
she seems like a ghost to Bigger. From the way Mrs. Dalton tou
the walls as she passes, Bigger can see that she is blind. Once ir
the office, Mr. Dalton interviews Bigger. Bigger answers the q
tions timidly, with few words apart from "yessuh" and "naws
He hates himself for acting in such a subservient manner, bu
cannot control himself and becomes extremely uncomfortable.

As Mr. Dalton continues to question Bigger, Mary Dalton—
Dalton's daughter and the girl from the newsreel—breezes int
room. The two are introduced, and Mary immediately asks Bi
if he belongs to a union. Bigger knows nothing about unions ex
that they are supposed to be bad, and he begins to hate Mary
endangering his chance at the job. Mary asks Mr. Dalton if she
be driven to the university for a lecture that evening. She then le
the room. Despite Bigger's worries, Mr. Dalton hires him as a ch
feur. Mr. Dalton tells Bigger that he is a great supporter of
NAACP—the National Association for the Advancement of C
ored People—and that he is hiring Bigger because of this supp
for blacks. Bigger's first assignment, Mr. Dalton says, is to di
Mary to the university that evening.

Peggy cooks dinner for Bigger, but he is suspicious of her ki
ness and thinks she may be trying to pass off some of her work o

profits from keeping blacks like Bigger's family in terrible housing, and expresses alleged benevolence by giving Bigger a menial job. We sense similar condescension in Mrs. Dalton's charity as well. Her charity is not unconditional, as she wants Bigger to do what *she* thinks he should want to do. The Daltons may give money to black schools, but they do not acknowledge that Bigger ultimately should have the freedom and opportunity to determine the course of his own life, without their interference.

Mrs. Dalton's blindness is important symbolically. Like Ralph Ellison's *Invisible Man, Native Son* includes many metaphors for race relations that relate to the concepts of vision and sight. Mrs. Dalton is literally blind, but also metaphorically blind: she and her husband are blind to Bigger's social reality. Bigger himself is similarly blinded by his hatred and fear. This blindness erects a dense wall of racial stereotypes between Bigger and the Daltons that prevents them from seeing each other as individual human beings. In Bigger's eyes, the Daltons represent "whiteness"—the overwhelming, hostile, and controlling force that imprisons him in a world of few choices, none of which appeals to him. To the Daltons, Bigger represents the mass of needy black Americans who can be exploited but can also be used as convenient targets of charitable giving. Though Mr. Dalton effectively robs Bigger and his family through artificially high rents, he alleviates any conscious or unconscious guilt about such robbery by making charitable donations toward black causes.

Indeed, the social divisions in *Native Son* are more clearly delineated along such lines of race than along lines of class. Though Peggy is a servant—and thus ostensibly Bigger's equal in terms of social class—she is just as patronizing to him as the Daltons are. Peggy's remark about "your people" demonstrates her belief that black Americans are foreigners or outsiders of some sort. Conversely, when Peggy refers to the Dalton household, she says "us." Though she is of a lower class than the Daltons, she clearly includes herself as one of "us," whereas she does not include Bigger and the previous black chauffeur. Although Peggy seems kind, she still considers herself superior to Bigger because she is white.

Bigger feels extremely uncomfortable when racial boundaries are crossed, as such situations represent unfamiliar territory. He reacts to Mary with hostility because she crosses the tense social boundary between white women and black men. In Bigger's limited experience, white women speak to him only from afar, with coldness and reserve. Mary, however, speaks to Bigger directly, which greatly confuses him. He thinks perhaps Mary might be trying to keep him from getting the job with the Daltons, as he is unable to comprehend the possibility that she might genuinely be interested in what he has to say. Complicating the situation is the fact that white women are utterly forbidden to black men. Though Mary is reaching out to Bigger, and not vice versa, Bigger knows that he would be the one to bear the blame should something go wrong. Mary thus terrifies and shames Bigger on many levels. He does not know how to behave in her presence because she breaks the only social rules he knows.

BOOK ONE (PART FOUR)

From driving Mary to meet Jan through Mary's death and the end of Book One

SUMMARY

> *He saw a hatchet.* Yes! *That would do it.*
>   (See QUOTATIONS, p. 62)

Stepping into the car, Mary informs Bigger that she is not going to the university, but instead has other plans that she does not want to reveal to her parents. Bigger agrees to keep Mary's activities a secret and guesses correctly that she plans to meet with some communists. Bigger grows increasingly anxious. He senses that Mary speaks to him as a human, an attitude he has never before encountered from a white person. Despite the freedom he feels with her, Bigger cannot forget that she is part of the world of people who tell him what he can and cannot do.

Mary introduces Bigger to her friend and lover, Jan Erlone, whom Bigger also recognizes from the newsreel. Jan confounds Bigger by shaking his hand and insisting that Bigger call him by his first name. Bigger thinks Mary and Jan are secretly making fun of him. He becomes infuriated because Mary and Jan make him intensely aware of his black skin—something he feels is a "badge of shame." Their attention makes him feel naked and ashamed, and he feels a "dumb, cold, and inarticulate hate" for them.

Jan insists on driving. Mary squeezes into the front seat beside Bigger, who feels surrounded by "two vast white looming walls." Bigger also intensely feels his physical proximity to a rich white girl, the smell of her hair, and the pressure of her thigh against his. Jan looks out at the city skyline and declares that "we" will own everything one day and that eventually there will be no black or white. Mary and Jan insist on eating at a black restaurant on the South Side. When pressed for a suggestion, Bigger offers Ernie's Kitchen Shack. As they drive to the restaurant, Mary looks at the apartment buildings in the black district and wistfully tells Bigger that she wants to know how black people live. She has never been inside a black household, but thinks their lives must not be so different—after all, "[t]hey're *human*. . . . They live in our country . . . [i]n the same city with us. . . ."

Mary and Jan insist that Bigger eat with them—a gesture that horrifies Bigger. They persist, however, so he angrily agrees. Mary begins to cry, sensing that she and Jan have made Bigger feel bad. Bigger feels trapped. He tries to think of what he would say to Mr. Dalton or the welfare agency if he were to walk off the job, but knows he cannot explain it. Jan comforts Mary and her tears are quickly forgotten as they go into the restaurant. Inside, Bigger encounters his girlfriend, Bessie, and his friend, Jack. When Bessie tries to talk to him, Bigger responds gruffly.

Jan, Mary, and Bigger eat dinner and then drink rum together. After a few drinks, Jan and Mary question Bigger about his history. He tells them that he grew up in Mississippi and that his father died in a riot. When Jan asks how he feels about his father's death, Bigger tells him that he does not know. Jan tells Bigger that the communists are fighting against this kind of injustice. Mary insists that she and Jan want to be Bigger's friends, and that he will get used to them. Bigger does not reply. Before they leave the restaurant, Mary tells Bigger she is going to Detroit at nine o'clock the next morning and that he should bring her small trunk to the station at eight-thirty.

Bigger drives Jan and Mary around the park while they make out in the back seat. The two have become thoroughly drunk by the time Bigger drops Jan off. Before he leaves, Jan gives Bigger some communist pamphlets to read. Mary, riding in the front seat next to Bigger, tries to engage in a conversation with him. She leans her head on his shoulder and asks him if he does not mind. She laughs, and again Bigger feels she is making fun of him. He again feels overcome by fear and hatred.

When Mary and Bigger arrive back at the Daltons', Mary is too drunk to walk unaided. Terrified, Bigger helps her into the house and up the stairs to her bedroom, leaving the car in the driveway. In the bedroom, Bigger becomes sexually aroused and kisses Mary. He lays Mary down on the bed and is groping her breasts when Mrs. Dalton suddenly enters the room. Bigger is seized by hysterical terror. He knows that Mrs. Dalton is blind, but he worries that Mary may say something that unwittingly reveals his presence. Mary starts to rise in response to her mother's voice, so Bigger places a pillow over Mary's face to prevent her from speaking. In his panic, he accidentally smothers Mary to death. Mrs. Dalton kneels by the bed and smells the alcohol on her daughter. She prays and returns to her bedroom.

Bigger realizes that Mary is dead and tries frantically to devise a plan. He stuffs her body into her trunk and carries it down to the basement. He stops in front of the furnace and decides to burn the body. He forces her body through the door, but her head will not fit, so he cuts it off with a hatchet and stuffs the rest of her remains into the furnace. Bigger decides that he will act as though nothing has happened and that he will take Mary's trunk to the station in the morning. When the Daltons realize their daughter is missing, Bigger will tell them that he accompanied her and Jan to her room to get her trunk. Bigger knows that the Daltons see Jan as a dangerous communist, and hopes that they will thus hold him responsible for Mary's disappearance. Bigger takes Mary's purse, which contains a wad of money, and hurries to his family's apartment on the South Side.

ANALYSIS

In this section we see that Mary Dalton is dangerously oblivious to the social codes that draw a strict boundary between white women and black men. She behaves as if social codes are merely silly prejudices to ignore, and does not realize that her actions could have serious consequences for Bigger. Jan likewise ignores these social codes, and inadvertently provokes terror, anger, and shame in Bigger. On the whole, Mary and Jan's attempts to treat Bigger as an equal only make him more conscious and ashamed of his black skin. Although Mary and Jan have good intentions in ignoring rules of conduct that they see as racist, Bigger nonetheless has good reason to fear and distrust their gestures. Though Jan requests that Bigger shake his hand and call him by his first name, Bigger knows that such actions would anger most white people, who would see them as disrespectful. Likewise, he knows that most other white people would be furious to see Bigger sitting in the front seat with Mary. Thus, as Mary and

Jan treat Bigger as an equal, they confuse him and unconsciously expose him to a frenzy.

Mary uses the same language as Peggy to describe black Americans. When talking to Bigger, she uses the phrase "your people." She refers to black Americans as "they" and "them," implying that blacks constitute a separate, essentially different class of human beings. Her phrase "our country" indicates that she views America as a nation dominated by white people. When Mary exclaims, "They're human," she implies that a psychological division exists between white and black Americans. She does not have the sensitivity to say "we're human" because she cannot include blacks and whites in the same collective. To her, the idea of being "human" means living like the white "us." We see, then, that though Mary has the best intentions and considers herself socially progressive, on an unconscious level she still sees blacks as separate or different.

Indeed, we see that Mary and Jan prove just as condescending as Mr. and Mrs. Dalton, even though they ascribe to radical political and social views and make a genuine effort to understand racial problems in America. Mary and Jan enjoy an odd yet titillating satisfaction from the act of eating at a black restaurant with Bigger. We get the sense that breaking social barriers is a sort of game to them. Though Mary and Jan want to experience black life, they do not even come close to an understanding of its most horrific aspects—the frustration and hopelessness Bigger feels every day. Like the Daltons, Mary and Jan remain blind to the social reality of what it means to be black. For a moment, it seems that Mary may recognize her blindness to Bigger's feelings. She weeps because she is ashamed that she has pushed Bigger against his will. Jan, however, lacks the sensitivity to recognize that he and Mary have placed Bigger in an awkward position, so this small window of understanding is quickly closed.

When Bigger finds himself in Mary's room, he knows he has breached the most explosive racial rule—the sexual separation between black men and white women. As Bigger puts Mary to bed, he becomes excited and aroused. This excitement comes not so much from the fact that Mary is physically attractive, but from his knowledge that she is forbidden to him. When Bigger feels Mrs. Dalton's ghostly presence in the room, he is reminded of the whiteness that controls his life, and is overcome by the magnitude of his transgression. Should Mrs. Dalton discover him, the horrible fate he has always expected for himself would surely be sealed forever.

Bigger once again finds his skin color trapping him in a situation in which the only option proves to be fatal.

Bigger's disposal of Mary's body is brutal, and Wright spares none of the gruesome details. Wright does not want Bigger to be seen as a traditional hero, but instead wants to emphasize the extreme pain and rage Bigger feels, which make him capable of such a terrible act. By explicitly describing Bigger's act of decapitating Mary's body, Wright shows that his protagonist is not a moral innocent. Racism has destroyed Bigger's innocence, awakening within him the capability to murder.

BOOK TWO (PART ONE)

From the opening of Book Two through Bigger leaving Mary's money with Bessie

SUMMARY

Bigger wakes up earlier than the rest of his family, and he is in a panic. He realizes he must get rid of Mary's purse as well as his own knife, which still has blood on the blade. Bigger finds the communist pamphlets Jan gave him and plans to use them as evidence against Jan if the police come around asking questions. When his mother wakes and asks why he did not get home until four o'clock in the morning, Bigger insists that he returned at two, because that time fits better with the story he has constructed. Bigger stares silently around him, infuriated and bewildered that his family has to live in such griminess. Vera accuses Bigger of staring at her and begins to sob as he tries to keep his composure.

Bigger contemplates his crime and becomes filled with a sense of invincibility. In murdering Mary, he feels he has created a new life for himself. He convinces himself that Mary's death is not accidental, but is actually something to which his whole life has been leading. Bigger feels a kind of pride in thinking that one day he will publicly accept what he has done. He decides that Jan, Mary, and the Daltons are blind, and, staring at his family, he realizes that they too are blind. Buddy longs to have a job like Bigger's, and Vera already shows the beginnings of the same weariness that marks his mother's face, exhibiting a profound fear of life in her every gesture.

As Bigger bounds down the stairs, Buddy calls after him, handing him a large wad of bills that has fallen out of Bigger's pocket. Bigger tells Buddy not to tell anyone about the money. Bigger then showily purchases cigarettes for Jack, G. H., and Gus before getting on a streetcar to go to the Daltons' home. Bigger begins to see that the white people around him are all blind. They see him as one who might steal, get drunk, or even rape, but they would never guess that he could be capable of murdering a white girl. Bigger marvels that he can act just as others expect him to, yet still do what he wants.

Bigger thinks of Mary and begins to believe that her murder is justified by the shame and fear that whites have caused him. White people, he thinks, are not really people, but a "great natural force." He wishes he could have a sense of solidarity with other black people to battle against this white force, but he knows such solidarity would only be achieved if blacks were forced into it out of desperation. Bigger thinks of Hitler in Germany and Mussolini in Italy, and wishes for some black leader to come along and whip black people into a group that would act together to "end fear and shame."

Bigger arrives at the Daltons' and finds Peggy peering into the furnace. For a moment he fears he may have to kill her, as the furnace is where he hid the body, but she sees nothing suspicious. Bigger adds coal to the furnace and leaves the unread communist pamphlets that Jan gave him in his room. Peggy sees that the car has been left outside all night, and Bigger tells her that Mary instructed him to leave it in the driveway. Peggy is skeptical, but Bigger mentions that a "gentleman" came to the Daltons' house the night before, and Peggy does not question him further. Bigger feigns surprise when Mary does not come down from her room, and Peggy suggests that perhaps Mary has already gone to the train station. Bigger delivers Mary's trunk to the station at 8:30. When Bigger returns, Jan calls looking for Mary.

Bigger is eager to watch the drama unfold. He eavesdrops on Peggy and Mrs. Dalton's worried conversation. Peggy mentions that Jan called to speak to Mary, and believes that Mary might have asked Jan to make the call in an attempt to cover something up. Mrs. Dalton becomes worried when Peggy says that it looks like Mary did not pack all her things. Bigger realizes that he did not think of this detail, and for the first time he feels nervous. Mrs. Dalton questions him, and he repeats his story, adding that Jan accompanied him to Mary's room. Mrs. Dalton gives Bigger the rest of the day off.

Bigger berates himself for somehow failing to acquire more money during the murder and cover-up, feeling that he should have planned things more carefully. He visits Bessie and shows her the money. Bessie tells Bigger that his employers live in the same section of town as the Loeb family. They discuss a recent case in which Richard Loeb and his friend Nathan Leopold kidnapped a neighborhood boy, killed him, and tried to collect ransom money from the family. Bigger remembers the case and begins to concoct his own ransom plan.

Bigger sees that Bessie is as blind as his family, as she uses liquor to blot out the pain of her life. He struggles over whether or not to trust her, but tells her that he has a big plan to obtain more money. Bigger tells Bessie that the Daltons' daughter ran away with a "Red," and that he took the money from Mary's room after she disappeared. He says he wants to write a ransom note and collect more. He assures Bessie that Mary has disappeared for good, but Bessie is suspicious of how he knows for certain. When Bessie asks Bigger if he is involved with Mary's disappearance, he threatens to beat her. He tells Bessie to retrieve the ransom money at a planned drop-off site, assuring her that he will be able to warn her if the money is marked or if the police are watching, as he works for the Daltons and will be privy to their plans. Bessie hesitantly agrees to help, so he gives her Mary's money for safekeeping.

ANALYSIS

Structurally, the opening of Book Two inaugurates a new phase of *Native Son* that corresponds with a turn in the novel's events. Mary's death represents a key turning point in the plot, both in terms of the narrative and in terms of Bigger's development as a character. In Book One, "Fear," Bigger is unable to analyze his behavior, aside from a few instances when he rationalizes his actions enough to forget them. In Book Two, "Flight," he begins to actively contemplate his identity and consciousness. At the beginning of the novel, Bigger writhes under the yoke of white authority, resentful of the line drawn between himself and white America. However, he does not cross this line until terror drives him to kill Mary by accident. Though this action threatens Bigger's life, it also, ironically, gives him a tangible goal: to get away with the murder. Bigger now feels the sense of clear purpose he lacks prior to killing Mary.

Bigger clearly still suffers from self-deception. Mary's death is an accident, but he convinces himself that it was a deliberate action on his part. To Bigger, the deliberate murder of a white woman represents the ultimate rebellion against the crushing authority of "whiteness." While he has in fact killed a white girl, Bigger convinces himself that he did not do so accidentally, but rather he consciously challenged and defeated the unfair social order imposed upon him. Given that Bigger does not have the ability to determine life and death, he feels that he now possesses a power that white America has used against him since his birth. In Bigger's fantasy, his alleged victory is an act of creation: he believes that killing Mary gives him a new life, one that he himself controls. Bigger sees framing Jan as merely the first step in constructing and protecting his new life. Through these actions, Bigger claims equality with whites on his own terms, and feels that he has become more human because his life now holds purpose. A bitter irony pervades this entire idea of life-affirming transformation, as the transformation occurs only after a brutal, irrational act of violence.

Bigger believes that blacks who simply accept the social order defined by white America are blinding themselves to the truth. His mother is blind because she depends on religion to cope with her disadvantaged position in life, and because she accepts the role she has been assigned despite the suffering it causes. Buddy views Bigger's menial job as an honorable position. In Bigger's eyes, Buddy's attitude means that Buddy accepts the subservient role white America has assigned him. Vera spends every minute of her life in fear, but accepts this fear as an inevitable part of her existence as a poor black girl. Additionally, Bigger sees Mary, Jan, and the Daltons as blind because he senses that they arrogantly assume that their knowledge of "blackness" can protect them.

Bigger's longing for a leader who can bring solidarity to the black community represents a warning on Wright's part. When Bigger looks to the fascist leaders of Italy and Germany, he finds much that he admires. He does not care whether these leaders are morally right or wrong, but only that they point to a possible avenue of escape from the white force that oppresses Bigger and the black community. Through the character of Bigger, Wright shows us that the conditions in 1930s America are ripe for fascism to flourish and that millions of oppressed people are waiting to unite behind a powerful and charismatic leader, regardless of that leader's moral character.

To disguise his identity as an unrepentant black murderer of a white woman, Bigger plays the expected role of the humble, ignorant, subservient black boy. In this sense, he is beginning to manipulate his identity to his advantage. The Daltons' racism blinds them to Bigger's role in Mary's death, as they are unable to imagine Bigger taking any action beyond the role that they have already assigned him. Bigger thus subverts racial stereotypes, using them as a form of resistance and protection against white authority.

Now that Bigger has broken the ultimate social barrier by killing a white woman, he no longer feels afraid to commit robbery against whites. Bigger's plan to collect a ransom from the Daltons is inspired by the real-life Leopold and Loeb case. In the 1920s, two bored, wealthy students from prominent Chicago families decided to commit what they considered the perfect crime. For months, Nathan Leopold and Richard Loeb planned to kidnap the child of a wealthy family. They killed the child to cover up their crime, and then planned to collect $10,000 in ransom money from the family. Leopold, however, accidentally dropped his glasses when disposing of the child's body, and this evidence led to his and Loeb's arrests, trials, convictions, and sentences to life imprisonment. Clarence Darrow, the defending attorney in the famous Scopes monkey trial, defended Leopold and Loeb. He argued that World War I had led to a cheapening of human life and that his clients had grown up in a world that learned to glorify violence. Darrow thus argued that Leopold and Loeb's environment had influenced their callous attitude toward human life. In legal terms, Leopold and Loeb's crime is more serious that Bigger's, as it was completely premeditated rather than accidental. However, Wright reminds us that it is unlikely that anyone in the 1930s would accept the possibility that a black man such as Bigger accidentally killed a white woman such as Mary.

BOOK TWO (PART TWO)

From Bigger returning to the Daltons' through his being questioned by the press

SUMMARY

> *Bigger knew the things that white folks hated to hear Negroes ask for; and he knew that these were the things the Reds were always asking for.*
> (See QUOTATIONS, p. 63)

As Bigger leaves Bessie, he feels confident because he has taken his life into his own hands for once. His secret knowledge that he murdered Mary wipes out his fear and relieves him from the invisible force that has been burdening him. Upon reaching the Daltons' home, Bigger checks the furnace. Seeing nothing of Mary's body, he adds more coal to the fire. Peggy informs him that Mr. Dalton wants him to pick up Mary's trunk at the station because she has not claimed it. The Daltons have also discovered that Mary has not arrived in Detroit. Mr. and Mrs. Dalton question Bigger again and he repeats his story.

When Bigger returns from the station, the Daltons introduce him to Britten, a private investigator they have hired. Britten doggedly questions Bigger, who remains timid and subservient and sticks to his story. Bigger is excited that, for the first time, he is in control, getting to "draw the picture for them" in the same manner that white people have always defined the situation for him.

Bigger tells Britten that he had not driven Mary to the university. He says that he performed the job Mary instructed him to do and that he kept it a secret because Mary told him to do so. Continuing in this self-deprecating vein, Bigger describes the events at the restaurant. When Britten asks whether Jan discussed communism at dinner, Bigger plays the role of the befuddled, simpleminded black boy. Bigger says that Jan, not Mary, told him to take the trunk downstairs and leave the car in the driveway. Again, Bigger says that he has not mentioned this detail before because Mary had instructed him to keep the events a secret.

Britten produces the pamphlets Bigger left in his room and accuses him of being a communist. Bigger is surprised that he, as a black man, would be accused of being Jan's partner. He convinces Mr. Dalton that he took the pamphlets because Jan, a white man, had insisted that he take them. Mr. Dalton tells Britten that they cannot hold Bigger responsible for Mary's disappearance. Britten is not so sure, and Bigger can see that the investigator thinks he must be guilty simply because he is black. Bigger offers to leave his job, but Mr. Dalton apologizes and asks him to stay on. Bigger goes to his room and eavesdrops on Mr. Dalton and Britten as they discuss him. Mr. Dalton says that Bigger is not a bad boy, but Britten claims that "a nigger's a nigger" and that they are all trouble. Bigger feels he has seen a thousand people just like Britten and believes that he knows how to deal with him.

Dalton and Britten bring Jan to the house for questioning, and he denies seeing Mary the night before. He changes his story when Britten confronts him with the pamphlets he gave Bigger. When Mr. Dalton offers him money to reveal Mary's whereabouts, Jan stalks out of the house. Bigger checks the furnace again and then hurries to tell Bessie about the new developments. Jan confronts him in the

street, but Bigger pulls out his gun and chases Jan off. Jan's innocence fills Bigger with terrible anger, and it takes a few minutes for
him to regain his composure.

Bigger chooses a building managed by Mr. Dalton's company
as the drop-off site for the ransom money. At Bessie's, he writes a
ransom note demanding $10,000. He signs it "Red" and includes
a drawing of a hammer and sickle. Bessie no longer wants to assist
Bigger. She accuses Bigger of killing Mary, and Bigger admits it,
saying it is okay because "[t]hey done killed plenty of us." Bessie
is terrified and begs Bigger not to involve her. Bigger tells her men-
acingly that he will not leave her behind and allow her to turn him
in. Bessie then feels resigned to her fate. Bigger shows her the
drop-off site and instructs her to return to the site at midnight the
following night.

Bigger slips the ransom note under the Daltons' front door and
checks the furnace again. Mr. Dalton reads the letter and calls Britten. Bigger eavesdrops while Peggy assures Britten that Bigger acts
just like most "colored boys." Britten questions Bigger again, asking questions about his feelings for white women. Bigger is careful
to continue his timid and ignorant act.

The press arrives at the Daltons'. The newspapers have already
printed a story about Jan's arrest in connection with Mary's disappearance, and the reporters snap photographs as Mr. Dalton
explains that he has received a ransom note for $10,000. Mr. Dal-
ton orders Jan to be released, but admits to the press that the ransom note is signed "Red" and that it contains the emblem of the
Communist Party. Jan, meanwhile, refuses to leave jail and
declares that he has witnesses to contradict Bigger's story, so the
reporters take an even greater interest in Bigger. They appear
delighted to hear that Bigger did not want to eat with Jan and Mary
at Ernie's. They want to print an article using Bigger to "prove"
that the "primitive Negro" does not want to be "disturbed by
white civilization."

ANALYSIS

Bigger's calculated manipulation of the prejudices of others reveals
his cleverness and allows him a new opportunity to create something of his own. Thinking that racist whites would never consider
a black man bold and intelligent enough to commit such a crime, he
deliberately plays into these racial stereotypes to keep them off his

tracks. The ease with which Bigger accomplishes this goal implies the severity of racial prejudices in America at the time. By merely playing the role of the ignorant black servant to a tee, Bigger fools Mr. Dalton, Britten, and even the reporters. He carefully directs suspicion at Jan by manipulating the wealthy whites' anticommunist prejudices as well. Bigger relishes the chance to control the narrative for the whites, shaping their reality as he wants, just as they have shaped it for him all of his life.

Though the blindness of the white characters is again evident in this section, we also begin to see more clearly that Bigger is largely blind as well. While Britten clearly stereotypes Bigger, Bigger also stereotypes Britten as merely one of thousands of white authority figures he has seen in his life. Indeed, Bigger is clearly still prone to self-deception. Just as he earlier hides behind his "wall" to endure fear and shame, he now does the same to avoid his guilt. Bigger attempts to blame Mary for bringing about her own death. When he finally does admit the murder to Bessie, he tries to convince himself that the murder is justified because whites have killed so many blacks in the past. When Jan confronts him, Bigger is overwhelmed by such guilt that he nearly shoots Jan and falls into a stupor for a few minutes before getting a hold of himself.

As Bigger's plan unfolds, morality becomes increasingly ambiguous and complex. Wright's depiction of Bigger's scheme suggests that, in a world complicated by racial hatred, it is not simple to identify right and wrong, even in the case of murder. Though Bigger kills Mary and then criminally plots against her family, it can be argued that neither of these events represents a moral action, as Bigger's accidental homicide is prompted by his fear that the Daltons' prejudice would lead them to assume that he intends to rape Mary. Considering the Daltons' reactions to Bigger's scheming following the murder, he may well have been right. Though Bigger has clearly committed a crime, Wright implies that he is not fully to blame for his actions following the murder. Bigger makes a conscious choice to lie and plots to injure the Daltons, but the mindset in which he makes those choices has been shaped by the social structure the Daltons and other whites help to perpetuate.

SUMMARY & ANALYSIS

BOOK TWO (PART THREE)

From Peggy asking Bigger to clean the furnace through Bigger's capture at the end of Book Two

SUMMARY

> *In all of his life these two murders were the most*
> *meaningful things that had ever happened to him.*
> (See QUOTATIONS, p. 64)

As the reporters stand around in the basement discussing the story, Peggy asks Bigger to clean the ashes out of the furnace. Bigger sifts some of the ashes into the lower bin and adds more coal, hoping that he will not have to take the ashes out until the reporters leave. However, the ashes still block the airflow, causing thick smoke to fill the basement. A reporter grabs a shovel and clears the ashes. When the smoke dissipates, several pieces of bone and an earring are visible on the floor. As Bigger looks at these remnants of his gruesome killing, all of his old feelings return: he is black and he has done wrong. He once again longs for a weapon so he can strike out at someone. While the reporters marvel over the glowing hatchet head in the furnace, Bigger sneaks up to his room and jumps out the window. It is snowing heavily and he lands hard, the snow filling his mouth, eyes, and ears.

Bigger rushes to Bessie's house to keep her from going to the drop-off site for the money. When Bigger explains that he accidentally killed Mary, Bessie tells him the authorities will think he has raped Mary and has murdered her to cover up the evidence. Bigger thinks back to the shame, anger, and hatred he felt that night. He thinks that he has committed rape, but to him, "rape" means feeling as if his back is against a wall and being forced to strike out to protect himself, whether he wants to or not. Bigger thinks that he commits a form of "rape" every time he looks at a white face.

Bessie packs some clothes and blankets before she and Bigger flee to an empty building to hide. She tells Bigger that she sees her life clearly and resents how much trouble he has caused her. After they make a bed out of the blankets, Bigger rapes Bessie. He realizes he cannot take her with him but cannot leave her behind either. After she falls asleep, he kneels over her with a brick. He hesitates for a moment, but, seeing images of Mrs. Dalton, of Mary burning, of Britten, and of the law chasing him, he brings the brick down on

Bessie's skull. He realizes that Bessie, with her crying and her insistence for liquor, would only slow him down in his flight. Bigger then dumps her body down an airshaft, realizing too late that he has forgotten to remove the big wad of money from her clothing.

Bigger sleeps uneasily during the night. Though he senses his impending doom, he still feels powerful. Like Mary's death, Bessie's death gives Bigger a newfound vigor, and he feels a sense of wholeness he has never felt before. In the morning, he awakes to a city covered in snow. He slips out to a street corner to steal a newspaper and reads the front-page news about his escape. The press reports that Bigger probably sexually assaulted Mary before killing her. The authorities have a warrant to search any and every building on the South Side, including private homes. Not believing that a black man could have formulated such a complex plan, they are also searching for a communist accomplice. White anger is turning on blacks and there are reports of smashed windows and beatings throughout the city.

Fighting hunger and cold, Bigger looks for a vacant apartment in which to hide. Due to the overcrowding caused by an alleged housing shortage on the South Side, he has to search for a long while before he finally finds a suitable place. From a window, Bigger marvels at the dilapidated buildings where black tenants live. He thinks back on his own life as he sees three naked black children watching their parents have sex in a bed nearby. He remembers how his family was once driven out of an apartment just two days before the building collapsed. Next door, Bigger hears two people debating his situation. One man declares that he would turn Bigger in to the police, while the other argues that Bigger may not be guilty, since whites automatically view all black men with suspicion when a white girl is killed. Still, the first man blames people like Bigger for bringing white wrath down on the whole black community.

The next morning, Bigger uses his last few pennies to purchase a newspaper. The police have searched over 1,000 black homes. Only a tiny square on the map—the place Bigger is hiding—remains untouched. The police have questioned or arrested numerous communists. A siren shrieks as the police arrive. Bigger escapes to the roof just as they burst into the building. A dramatic shoot-out ensues and the authorities finally capture Bigger, who is half-frozen from the cold and snow. The men carry Bigger down as a crowd of furious whites demands that they kill "that black ape."

[N]ever in all his life, with this black skin of his, had the two worlds, thought and feeling, will and mind, aspiration and satisfaction, been together. . . .

(See QUOTATIONS, p. 65)

ANALYSIS

As Bigger goes on the run, fear and guilt continue to torment him. Though Mary's murder is an accident, Bessie's is not. Bigger is tormented by his consciousness of how wrong this second killing is, even at the moment he is committing it. In order to go through with the terrible act, he has to imagine the white blur he feels hovering near him on the night he kills Mary. Bigger forces himself to remember the horror of Mary's burning corpse, Britten's racist hatred, and the police who are closing in on him. While Bigger has already allowed his previously repressed fear and anger to come to the surface, he now must contend with his repressed feelings of guilt. He cannot bear to look at Bessie's face, fearing that she will look at him accusingly even in death, just as Jan does when confronting Bigger in the street. Bigger fears the onslaught of an unstoppable feeling of guilt that would destroy him just as fear and anger have threatened to in the past. Bigger feels such a great need to repress his guilt that he prefers to leave all his money with Bessie's body rather than face her again.

To some degree, Bigger is able to distract himself from his guilt by concentrating on the new sense of power he feels after doing something significant for the first time in his life. The murders give Bigger a chance to "live out the consequences of his actions," freeing him from the image of blackness that white America has imposed upon him and giving him a chance to control his own fate. Ironically, Bigger has had to murder in order to gain that control, and he only feels freedom at a time when he is trapped in the city with the police closing in on him.

Bigger's flight from the police during the blizzard can be interpreted as a metaphor for his entire life. He is literally corralled by the relentless manhunt, as the forces of "whiteness" pursue him in an intense building-by-building search of the entire South Side. Like a cornered rat, Bigger is trapped within the ever shrinking square of space that the police have not yet searched. The snowstorm is a literal symbol of the metaphorical "whiteness" that Bigger fears. The snow encompasses and impedes Bigger, shutting down the city and preventing his escape from the white manhunt. Like the waves of white men searching for him, the snow falls relentlessly around Bigger, locking him in place. Literally and symbolically, "whiteness" falls on Bigger's head with the power of a natural disaster.

During his flight into the black South Side, Bigger takes time to look at the conditions in which he has lived, and realizations dawn on him as if he is seeing these conditions for the first time. The image of the naked children watching as their parents have sex is a reminder of the shame Bigger felt growing up. He sees that real estate owners like Mr. Dalton have forced black tenants to crowd into one small section of the city, creating an artificial housing shortage that drives rents up. Though Bigger's social consciousness has clearly grown throughout the novel, he is only beginning to understand the broader picture of the complex racial conflict in American society.

BOOK THREE (PART ONE)

From the opening of Book Three through Bigger signing his confession

SUMMARY

In jail, Bigger lives in a world with no day, no night, and no fear or hatred, as such emotions are useless to him now. He feels gripped by a deep resolution to react to nothing, and he says and eats nothing. He longs for death, but as a black man he does not want to die "unequal, and despised." Bigger wonders if perhaps the whites are right that being black is the same as being an animal of some sort. Nonetheless, the hope that another way of life exists, one in which he would be able to forget his racial differences, keeps coming back to him.

The authorities drag Bigger to an inquest at the morgue. He senses from the white people around him that they plan not only to put him to death, but also to make him a symbol to terrorize and control the black community. A feeling of rebellion rises in him and he begins to come out of his stupor. In the morgue, Bigger sees Jan and the Daltons. As he gradually begins to snap out of his psychological stupor, he faints, overcome by hunger and exhaustion. When Bigger awakens in his cell, he believes he has "come out into the world again" in order to save his pride and keep the authorities from "making sport of him."

Bigger asks to see a newspaper. The headline reads, "Negro Rapist Faints at Inquest." The story compares Bigger to a "jungle beast" who lacks the harmless charm of the "grinning southern darky." Edward Robertson, editor of the *Jackson Daily Star*, advises total segregation and a curtailment of the education of the black population, which he claims will prevent men like Bigger from developing. Bigger contemplates returning to his protective stupor, but is not sure if he is still able to do so.

Reverend Hammond, the pastor of Mrs. Thomas's church, visits Bigger in his cell. The Reverend talks to him about hope and love beyond life. Bigger feels a terrible guilt for having killed within himself the kind of world the preacher describes. He compares the murder of his faith to his murder of Mary. Hammond places a cross around Bigger's neck just as Jan enters the cell. Jan says that he is not angry and that he wants to help Bigger. Jan says he was foolish to assume that Bigger could have related to him in a different way than he relates to other white men. Jan says that he loved Mary, but he also realizes that black families loved all the black men who have been sold into slavery or lynched by whites. As Jan speaks, Bigger notes that this moment is the first time in his life that he has seen a white person as an individual human being, rather than merely a part of the larger oppressive force of whiteness. This feeling deepens Bigger's guilt, as he knows he has killed the woman Jan loved. Jan introduces Bigger to Boris A. Max, a lawyer for the Labor Defenders. Max wants to defend Bigger free of charge.

Buckley, the State's Attorney, suddenly enters Bigger's cell. Though Max argues that white power is responsible for Bigger's actions, Bigger feels his burgeoning friendship with Max and Jan quickly evaporate when he sees the self-assured Buckley. Mr. and Mrs. Dalton enter the cell and ask that Bigger cooperate with Buckley and reveal the name of his accomplice. In response, Max asks that they not sentence Bigger to death. Dalton says that despite the crime he is not angry with all black Americans. He announces that he has even sent some Ping-Pong tables to the South Side Boys' Club earlier in the day. Doubtful, Max questions whether Ping-Pong will prevent murder.

Bigger's family and his friends Jack, G. H., and Gus enter the now crowded cell. Bigger looks at them and thinks they should be glad that he has "taken fully upon himself the crime of being black," and thus washed away their shame. He knows, however, that they still feel shame, and he asks his mother to forget him. Mrs.

Thomas tearfully begs the Daltons to have mercy, but they only reply that they have no control over the matter. Mrs. Thomas also tells Mr. Dalton that his real estate company has been trying to evict her family, and he promises they will not be evicted.

All the visitors leave the cell except Buckley, who warns Bigger not to gamble with his life by trusting Max and Jan. Buckley shows Bigger the mob gathered outside, which is screaming for his blood and urging him to sign a confession that also implicates Jan. Adding that the authorities know Bigger raped and killed Bessie too, Buckley pressures him to confess to other unsolved rapes and murders. Bigger realizes he could never explain why he killed Mary and Bessie because it would mean explaining his whole life. Bigger confesses to the murders but writes nothing to explain them. He signs his confession, feeling that there is no alternative. As soon as Bigger signs, Buckley starts to brag about how easy it was to extract a confession from a "scared colored boy from Mississippi." After Buckley leaves, Bigger, feeling empty and beaten, falls to the floor and sobs.

ANALYSIS

As Bigger retreats into himself, the white authorities and press take control over his identity once again, redefining him as a bestial Negro rapist and murderer. Wright's influence for this treatment of Bigger's character may have come from actual events. While writing the novel, Wright studied newspaper clippings from the 1938 Chicago murder trial of Robert Nixon, a young black man who killed a white woman with a brick during a robbery. Wright used many details from those articles, especially the descriptions of Nixon as an animal, in his writing of *Native Son*.

The whites attempt to reshape Bigger's identity with these additional gruesome details not only to demonize Bigger, but also to whip up white violence and terrorize the black community into submission. Edward Robertson's newspaper editorial blames northern whites for giving blacks too many opportunities, but also implicitly warns the black community to behave or risk a return to the kind of oppression many of them have left behind in the South. This awareness that whites are attempting to use him as a lesson to the black world angers Bigger and prevents him from staying in his insulated, catatonic state. Sensing that his back is once again up against the wall, he feels a renewed sense of rebellion and comes to be ready—though, as always, not completely willing—to fight.

In jail, we see Bigger grapple with conflicting and often unwanted visions of hope. Alone in his cell, he has visions of a new identification with the world, a way to merge with men and women around him and become part of a community. He tries to shake this image from his mind because, given his current situation, hope only makes him feel worse. Reverend Hammond confronts Bigger with another kind of hope, the same spiritual hope that his mother's religion promises. The reverend tells Bigger tales of the world beyond life, but Bigger knows he has killed this faith in himself long ago. He does, however, take the cross to wear and seems to take some solace in the reverend's words. He even thinks of himself as Christlike in the presence of his family and friends. Just as Christian tradition maintains that Jesus died to wash away the sins of the world, Bigger has "taken fully upon himself the crime of being black" and will die to wash away the shame blacks have experienced.

Jan's arrival in the cell marks an important moment in the novel. In his initial encounter with Jan, on the night of Mary's murder, Bigger senses that Jan and Mary are trying to speak to him as a man. Nonetheless, their blindness to Bigger's feelings makes any connection between them impossible. Now, however, Jan understands what Bigger felt the night he murdered Mary. Jan tells Bigger that he realizes he acted blindly toward Bigger that night, and thus in a way is somewhat responsible for Mary's murder. The terrible act has allowed Jan, just like Bigger, to see things more clearly. Jan becomes the first white man Bigger sees as an individual, rather than merely a representation of the whiteness that Bigger has felt pressing down on him.

The crowd that gathers in the jail cell requires us to suspend our disbelief. It seems unlikely that so many people would be allowed, let alone actually fit, inside an accused murderer's cell. Wright tried to deflect this criticism by explaining that he was more interested in the emotional truth of the scene than he was in its physical reality. The crowd of individual visitors represents the collective voice of society as it reacts to and judges Bigger's case. Mrs. Thomas's voice cries for mercy, while Buddy is ready to take revenge. The Daltons speak with the voice of condescending liberalism, intent on revenge but unable to acknowledge the role they have played in creating Bigger's frame of mind. Finally, Buckley represents the voice of white power and racism, convinced Bigger is less than human and eager to make him a symbol for other blacks who might dare to cross the line Bigger has crossed.

BOOK THREE (PART TWO)

From the inquest through Bigger's meeting with Max

SUMMARY

The authorities lead Bigger to the courtroom for the inquest. Mrs. Dalton testifies that the earring found in her furnace is a family heirloom that she had given to Mary. She states that she and her husband have donated millions of dollars to black schools. Jan follows Mrs. Dalton to the stand. During questioning, the coroner insinuates that Jan promised Bigger sex with white women if Bigger joined the Communist Party. Max argues that these kinds of questions are sensational and designed only to inflame public opinion, but his objections are overruled.

Mr. Dalton takes the stand and Max is permitted to question him. As Max knows that Mr. Dalton owns a controlling share in the company that manages the building where Bigger's family lives, he asks Dalton why black tenants pay higher rents than whites for the same kinds of apartments. Dalton replies that there is a housing shortage on the South Side. Max retorts that there are areas of the city without housing shortages, and Dalton replies that he thought black tenants preferred living together on the South Side. Max then succeeds in making Dalton admit that he refuses to rent to black tenants in other neighborhoods. He accuses Dalton of giving some of the real estate profits to black schools merely to alleviate his guilty conscience. Before dismissing Mr. Dalton, Max asks him if the living conditions of Bigger's family might have contributed to the death of his daughter. Dalton cannot comprehend the question.

The coroner exhibits Bessie's body to the jurors. Bigger knows that the authorities are using Bessie only to ensure that he will get the death penalty for killing Mary. Bigger becomes angry that they are using Bessie in death just as Bessie's white employer used her while she was alive. He feels that the whites are using both him and Bessie as if they were mere property.

Bigger is indicted for rape and murder. When the police take him to the Dalton home and ask him to reenact the crime, he backs himself against the wall and refuses. Outside, a mob screams for his death. Bigger sees a burning cross across the street. He feels that Hammond, in giving him the cross to wear, has betrayed him: the preacher has made him feel a kind of hope, but the burning cross leaves him hopeless once again. Back in his jail cell, Bigger rips off the cross and flings it away. When Hammond tries to visit him again, Bigger furiously refuses him. He vows never to trust anyone again.

Bigger asks to see a newspaper, which reports that he is certain to receive the death penalty. A hysterical black prisoner is brought to Bigger's cell, demanding the return of his papers. Another prisoner tells Bigger that this hysterical prisoner went crazy from studying too much at a university. The man had been trying to understand why blacks were treated so badly and had been picked up at the post office, where he was waiting to speak to the president. His screaming disturbs other prisoners, and he is taken away on a stretcher.

Max visits Bigger in his cell. Hopeless, Bigger tells Max that none of his efforts will be of use. Bigger feels destined to die to appease the public, and, therefore, has no possibly of winning the trial. Max tries to get Bigger to trust him. Despite his best efforts to avoid opening up and trusting anyone, Bigger does end up trusting Max, but still believes Max's efforts will prove futile. Max then asks Bigger why he killed Mary. Excited at the prospect of finally feeling understood, Bigger tells Max that he did not rape Mary and hints that he killed her by accident. When Max presses him further about his feelings, Bigger states that Mary's unorthodox behavior frightened and shamed him. When Max points out that Bigger could have avoided the murder by trying to explain himself to Mrs. Dalton, Bigger explains that he could not help himself and that it was as if someone else had stepped inside him and acted for him.

Bigger explains to Max that there has always been a line drawn in the world separating him from the people on the other side of the line, who do not care about his poverty and shame. He says that whites do not let black people do what they want, and admits that he himself does not even know what he wants. Bigger simply feels that he is forbidden from anything he might actually want. All his life, he has felt that whites were after him. Thus, even his feelings were not wholly his own, as he could only feel what whites were doing to him. Bigger once wanted to be an aviator, but he knew that black men were not allowed to go to aviation schools. He wanted to join the army, but it proved to be segregated and based upon racist laws. He saw the white boys from his school go on to college or the military when he could not. Having lost hope, he began living from day to day. Bigger says that after he killed Mary and Bessie, he ceased to be afraid for a brief while.

Bigger snorts at the idea that the Daltons think they have changed something by donating Ping-Pong tables to the South Side

Boys' Club, as he and his friends planned most of their robberies while hanging around the Club. Bigger says the church did not help him either, as it preached happiness only in the afterlife while he longed for happiness in this world. He also believes that once he is executed, there will be no afterlife. Bigger tells Max that he took a chance and lost, but that it is over now and he does not want anyone to feel sorry for him. Max decides to enter a plea of "not guilty" to buy some time to plead Bigger's case.

ANALYSIS

The brief appearance of a crazed inmate in Bigger's cell gives us another example of the narrow range of choices with which Bigger has grown up. We have seen some of these limited choices already: Bigger's mother attempts to get by with religion and the hope for a better life beyond this world; Bessie relies on alcohol and dancing to ease her pain; and Bigger retreats behind his wall, lashing out violently when pushed too far. With the mad inmate, Wright shows us the danger of another option: attempting to tackle the problems of race relations using pure reason. The former student is driven mad by looking at the race problem closely and trying to understand the situation of blacks in America. Wright implies that approaching the situation rationally is as dangerous as lashing out with a gun—and, in some ways, less effective.

Though Bigger feels the injustice of his situation intensely, he is uneducated and inarticulate, and therefore sometimes unable to convey his feelings adequately. Although his understanding becomes clearer as the novel moves on, he still struggles—even within his own thoughts—for a way to describe his world. Wright sidesteps these limitations of Bigger's character by creating the character of the mad student, who is intelligent enough to be able to voice his own philosophical perspectives on Bigger and the world that has created him. Furthermore, at the inquest, Max is able to make explicit the hypocrisy of the Daltons and their charity, something Bigger has sensed but has not expressed outright. As a white man, Max is also able to attack Dalton directly, something a black man in Wright's Chicago would not have done. Max mocks Dalton's pathetic gesture of benevolence—his gift of Ping-Pong tables to the Boys' Club—and makes clear that Dalton is a major part of a system that corrals black tenants into the ghetto, creating the social conditions that have produced Bigger. Dalton is blind to these allegations, just as he is to Max's assertion that his role in creating these conditions makes him complicit in Mary's murder.

It is clear that the authorities do not consider Bessie's rape and murder to be as important as the murder of Mary Dalton. They use Bessie's battered body merely as evidence to establish the larger crime, which, in the eyes of the public, is the outrageousness of Bigger's act against white society. We get the impression that Bigger's trial is only a sensational spectacle for the public, and not an attempt to serve justice. The authorities' attempts to force Bigger to reenact his crime in Mary's bedroom reinforce this interpretation of the trial. We see that such ostensible evidence gathering is largely pointless, as Bigger's guilt has been decided before he is ever arrested. Instead, the reenactment serves only to provide sensational photographs to print in the next racist news article about the trial.

Max's acknowledgement of Bigger as a human being allows Bigger to talk—and even think—about himself in ways he never has before. Throughout *Native Son,* Wright focuses on this idea that physical oppression leads to psychological repression. Bigger has spent his entire life trying to hide behind a wall, attempting to shut out the realities of life and his feelings about these grim realities. Such repression has left him with violence as his only outlet. Max, however, by simply recognizing Bigger's life and feelings, allows Bigger to shed this burden of repression that he has carried for so long. Bigger can now, at least tentatively, emerge from behind his wall and start to examine his world for what it really is.

Book Three (Part Three)

From Bigger struggling with his feelings after his meeting with Max through the completion of the prosecution's testimony in court

Summary

Bigger is seized with nervous energy, filled with both hope and doubt. Max's questions have made Bigger feel that Max acknowledges his life and feelings. Bigger wonders if people on the other side of the "line" suffer from the same hatred and fear that have gripped him all of his life. He realizes that individual people, just like himself and Jan, comprise both sides of the color line. Bigger suddenly wishes to know more about life. He wants to touch the hands of people locked in other cells, both in prison and out in the world. He wants to feel the pain of others who suffer like him.

However, Bigger knows that he faces the death penalty, and therefore believes that it is too late to learn the meaning of his existence. He wishes he could retreat back into his mental stupor. He has a newfound feeling of hope for a new world and a new way of viewing himself in relation to other people, but this hope is tantalizing and torments him with uncertainty. Bigger wonders if perhaps his blind hatred is the better option anyway, since hope anguishes him more than it comforts him. The voice of hatred he has read in the newspapers seems so much louder and stronger than the voice of understanding he has heard in Max and Jan. Bigger despairs that this hatred will endure long after he is dead.

Bigger's family, friends, and teachers are in the courtroom for the trial. He wonders why the authorities do not just shoot him instead of forcing him to go through this long, public process. Max enters a guilty plea and explains that the law allows him to enter mitigating evidence for his defendant. Buckley claims that Max wants to plead guilty and then try to prove that Bigger is insane, which is not allowed under the law. Max denies this claim and says that he merely wants to demonstrate why Bigger has committed murder. Max accuses Buckley of rushing the trial to gain political advantage for the upcoming elections and claims that Buckley is merely a stooge who is doing the bidding of the mob that has gathered outside the courtroom. Max claims that Buckley wants to avoid the matter of motive because it would mitigate Bigger's punishment. The judge allows Max to do as he has planned, and the sentencing hearing begins.

Buckley calls Mr. and Mrs. Dalton, Peggy, and Britten to testify that Bigger behaved like a sane man. Next on the stand are the reporters who discovered Mary's bones in the furnace, followed by a parade of people who knew Bigger in the South Side. The theater manager testifies that Bigger and other boys had masturbated in the theater. Buckley even brings the Daltons' furnace into the courtroom. He presents his case over the course of two days.

ANALYSIS

Native Son is filled with dramatic action—there are two murders, a police chase, a shoot-out, and a murder trial—yet the most dramatic turmoil occurs inside Bigger's mind. In perhaps the most important moment in the novel, Bigger is suddenly able to see himself in relation to other people. Thanks to his discussion with Max, he now feels free from the tensions of his life. He no longer sees whites as just a "looming mountain of hate," but rather as individuals. Bigger has already seen Jan in this manner, but he now reaches the important realization that even those whites who hate him are human. In fact, if Bigger were in their place, he realizes he would likely hate in the same way that they do. This revelation has required Bigger to accept two important things: not only must he realize that whites are human beings, but he must also recognize that he himself is their equal. Previously, Bigger has been afraid even to think of himself in these terms. Now, however, the burdens of fear, hate, and shame have been lifted from him, and he is able to see that the problems of his life are not his alone. He imagines everyone—white and black, rich and poor—trapped alone in his or her own jail cell, longing for connection.

Bigger finally begins to realize that he has been just as blind as everyone else. Just as racist whites are blind to his humanity, he has been blind to the fact that Jan and Mary are human beings as well. He makes the crucial realization that the hatred and fear that drive people on the other side of the "line" to make a spectacle of him and wish him dead are the same kind of hatred and fear that he has felt himself. Bigger longs to overcome his alienation and become involved in the lives of others.

Bigger's awakening to the possibility of a connection with others represents a new source of hope. He has left religion behind because it only offers hope in the afterlife, but now he has found beliefs that enable him to see hope in this world. He imagines being able to reach out and touch the hearts of others around him. He feels that in his recognition of others, and their recognition of him, he can gain the identity and wholeness for which he has longed. Earlier, Bigger thinks that he has found this identity in his new status as a murderer, but that status leaves him tormented by guilt. This new identity brings Bigger an image of himself standing in a crowd of men in a blinding sun that has burned away all differences—not only differences of race, but of class as well.

Bigger struggles with the inner conflict produced by this new hope, and knows he must reconcile his new hope with the certainty that he will be sentenced to death. In the face of death, such hope is a torment. Bigger now longs for more time to examine and understand his relation to others. His new fear is that he will die before he has time to reach this understanding fully. He also feels defenseless in the face of ongoing hatred, despairing that the voices of hate will drown everything else out and continue long after he is dead. The mobs and the newspapers continue to call Bigger a monster, and he wonders if it is not better to hide again behind his wall of hate. Fighting this battle within himself, he realizes that to win the battle for his life on the outside he must first win it on the inside. This realization represents the end of the split consciousness from which Bigger has suffered throughout the novel. His newfound wholeness, although something he only barely understands, gives him the power to achieve victory in a sense, regardless of the outcome of his trial.

BOOK THREE (PART FOUR)

From the beginning of Max's speech through the end of the novel

SUMMARY

In the courtroom, Max presents his case. He argues that Bigger is a "test symbol" who embodies and exposes the ills of American society. Max explains that his intent is not to argue whether an injustice has been committed, but to make the court understand Bigger and the conditions that have created him. Max points out that the authorities have deliberately inflamed public opinion against Bigger, using his case as an excuse to terrorize the black community, labor groups, and the Communist Party into submission.

Max goes on to say that the rage directed at Bigger stems from a mix of guilt and fear. Those who clamor for Bigger's swift execution secretly know that their own privileges have been gained through historical wrongs committed against people like Bigger, and that their wealth has been accumulated through the oppression of others. Bigger's options have been so limited, and his life so controlled, that he has been unable to do anything but hate those who have profited from his misery. Stunted and deformed by this oppression, Bigger was unable to view Mary and Jan as human beings. Max argues that the Daltons, despite their philanthropy, are blind to the world that has created Bigger and have themselves created the conditions that led to their daughter's murder.

Max warns that killing Bigger quickly will not restrain others like him. Rather, these other blacks will only become angrier that the powerful, rich, white majority limits their opportunities. Popular culture dangles happiness and wealth before the oppressed, but such goals are always kept out of reach in reality. Max argues that this smoldering anger born out of restricted opportunities—though now tempered by the effects of religion, alcohol, and sex—will eventually burst forth and destroy all law and order in American society. By limiting the education of blacks, segregating them, and oppressing them, white society itself is implicated in Mary's murder. Max claims that white society "planned the murder of Mary Dalton" but now denies it. He says that his job is to show how foolish it is to try to seek revenge on Bigger.

Max argues that Bigger murdered Mary accidentally, without a plan, but that he accepted his crime, which gave him the opportunities of choice and action, and the sense that his actions finally meant something. Bigger's killing was thus not an act against an individual, but a defense against the world in which Bigger has lived. Mary died because she did not understand that she alone could not undo hundreds of years of oppression. Max points to the gallery, where blacks and whites are seated in separate sections. Blacks, he says, live in a separate "captive" nation within America, unable to determine the course of their own lives. He argues that such a lack of self-realization is just as smothering and stunting as physical starvation. Bigger sought a new life, Max says, and found it accidentally when he murdered Mary. Max argues that Bigger had no motive for the crimes and that the murders were "as instinctive and inevitable as breathing or blinking one's eyes." The hate and fear society has bred into Bigger are an inextricable part of his personality, and essentially his only way of living.

Max says that there are millions more like Bigger and that, if change does not come, these conditions could lead to another civil war. He says he knows the court does not have the power to rectify hundreds of years of wrongs in one day, but that it can at least show that it recognizes that there is a problem. Prison, he says, would be a step up for Bigger. Though Bigger would be known only as a number in prison, he would at least have an identity there. Finally, Max argues that the court cannot kill Bigger because it has never actually recognized that he exists. He urges the court to give Bigger life. Bigger does not entirely understand Max's speech, but is proud that Max has worked so hard to save him.

After Max's arguments, Buckley declares that Bigger does in fact have a motive for Mary's murder. Buckley claims that since Bigger and Jack masturbated while watching a newsreel about Mary the same day she was killed, Bigger must have been sexually interested in her. Buckley tells the courtroom that Bigger was a "maddened ape" who raped Mary, killed her, and burned her body to hide the evidence. Buckley concludes his argument by saying that Bigger was sullen and resentful from the start, not even grateful when he was referred to Mr. Dalton for a job. Buckley calls Bigger a "demented savage" who deserves to die, and whose execution will prove that "jungle law" does not prevail in Chicago. The court adjourns. After a brief deliberation, the judge returns and sentences Bigger to death.

Max visits Bigger again after a failed attempt to obtain a pardon from the governor. Bigger tries to explain how much Max's questions about his life meant to him, as these questions acknowledged Bigger's existence as a human being, even as a murderer. Max tries to comfort Bigger, but Bigger wants understanding, not pity. He continues, saying that sometimes he wishes Max had not asked the questions, because they have made him think and this thinking has scared him. The questions have made Bigger consider himself and other people in a new way, and have caused him to realize that his motivation for hurting people was simply that they were always crowding him. He did not mean to hurt others, but it just happened. When Bigger committed the murders, he was not trying to kill anyone, but rather to make his life mean something that he could claim for himself. Bigger asks Max if this sense of meaning is the same reason that the authorities want to kill him. Max urges his client to die free, believing in himself. He tells Bigger that only his own mind stands in the way of believing in himself. The rich majority dehumanizes people like Bigger for the same reason Bigger could not see the majority as human—they each just want to justify their own lives.

Bigger tells Max he does believe in himself. He did not want to kill, but there was something in him that has made him kill and that something must be good. He tells Max that he feels all right when he looks at it this way. Max is horrified at Bigger's words, but Bigger assures him that he is all right. Max bids him good-bye and as he leaves, Bigger asks him, "Tell . . . Tell Mister . . . Tell Jan hello."

ANALYSIS

In his long courtroom speech, Max articulates much of what Bigger has already seen and felt throughout the novel. He reiterates the Daltons' blindness and Bigger's blindness toward Mary and Jan. He tells the court how the murders gave Bigger the identity he lacked and how the hate and fear that Bigger's living conditions bred into him made the murders almost inevitable. While much of Max's speech simply restates what we have seen before, it does clarify the warning Wright implies with the ringing of the alarm clock at the novel's opening. Max worries that the same doom Bigger dreads in Book One is the fate of the entire country. Max appeals to the court—as Wright appeals to his readers in 1930s America—to recognize Bigger Thomas, to understand the conditions that have created him, and to comprehend the disastrous consequences of allowing these conditions to continue.

Many critics have argued that Wright uses Max's speech merely to expose his own communist propaganda. Others, however, have pointed out that Max, though a lawyer for the Communist Party, is never identified as a member of the Party himself. Also, Max's argument does not follow the party line exactly. Max does make clear that blacks have been oppressed for hundreds of years, and details the conditions under which they are forced to live in 1930s Chicago. His argument does not, however, appear to be a call for revolution or an attack on capitalism. Instead, Max makes an appeal to the rich and powerful simply to understand that they are sowing the seeds for a new civil war in continuing their oppression of blacks. In the end, Max, as a representative of the Communist Party, cannot save Bigger. Bigger learns that salvation can come only from within, through his own effort.

In a novel filled with characters who are blind both literally and metaphorically, Max sees the most clearly. He is able to understand and articulate much of Bigger's life after only one long conversation with him. Max sees that Bigger views whites not as individuals, but as a great natural force. He understands Bigger's split consciousness and sees how Bigger was forced to retreat from reality. He also understands how Mary's murder gave Bigger the chance to control his own life for the first time. For all his perceptiveness, however, Max is still unable to see Bigger completely. At the trial, he refers to Bigger as a symbol and talks of the millions more who are like him. In this statement, we see that Max understands Bigger, but that he cannot see Bigger beyond his own conception of who Bigger must be. When Bigger tells Max that he is pleased with what he has done, Max is unable to accept this assertion and gropes for his hat "like a blind man." Even Max is unable, ultimately, to see Bigger fully for the individual he is.

Critics, such as James Baldwin in *Everybody's Protest Novel,* have argued that Bigger goes to his death fearful and desperate, just like the rat in the first pages of the novel. Others contend that Bigger finally gives himself over to hatred. Nonetheless, it is important to note that Bigger does change in jail, accepting that the acts he has committed are part of who he is, but also that hate for one's oppressors is a natural feeling. It is the repression of these feelings—a repression Bigger has forced upon himself in order to survive—that leads to his violent acts. By the end of the novel, he has shed his hate and fear, and longs only to understand his place in the world and his relation to other people. Bigger tells Max again and again that he is all right. Finally, as Max is leaving, Bigger asks him to "[t]ell Jan hello." As Jan requests in the beginning of the novel, Bigger finally calls him by his first name, signifying that he finally sees whites as individuals, rather than a looming force. Even more important, Bigger sees himself as the whites' equal. Max exhorts Bigger to believe in himself, and we have every indication at this point to believe that he already does.

IMPORTANT QUOTATIONS EXPLAINED

1. Was what he had heard about rich white people really
    true? Was he going to work for people like you saw in
    the movies . . . ? He looked at *Trader Horn* unfold and
    saw pictures of naked black men and women whirling
    in wild dances . . . .

This passage from Book One appears as Bigger sits in the movie theater, thinking about the possibilities for his new job as the Daltons'
chauffeur. He has just seen the newsreel about Mary and has decided
that he might find more to like about the job than he initially sus-
pects. Here we see just how little contact Bigger has had with white
people and therefore how impossible it is for him to conceive of them
in realistic terms. We also see the importance of popular culture in
determining societal attitudes, as Bigger is only able to imagine the
Daltons' lives by drawing upon movies that portray rich white people. The movie screen shows a scene of black savages dancing in a
jungle, which Bigger covers up in his mind with an imagined scene of
an elegant white cocktail party. Wright juxtaposes these sharply con-
trasting images to indicate the extent to which Bigger's—and America's—attitudes about whites and blacks are determined by popular
culture. This popular culture inundates the America of Wright's time
with imagery that depicts blacks as savages and whites as cultured
and sophisticated millionaires.

2. The head hung limply on the newspapers, the curly black hair dragging about in blood. He whacked harder, but the head would not come off. . . . He saw a hatchet. *Yes!* That would do it. . . .

This extremely disturbing passage from the end of Book One describes Bigger's brutal disposal of Mary's body after he accidentally smothers her to death. He tries to stuff the body in the furnace, but the head will not fit, so he is forced to decapitate Mary in order to fit her corpse into the fire. The grisliness of this passage is intentional, and important to the novel: Wright does not want to portray Bigger as a passive victim of a situation beyond his control. He spares no gruesome detail, depicting Bigger's excited, racing mind and the gory work of dismembering Mary. Though there are extenuating social and personal circumstances surrounding Mary's death, Wright does not want to portray Bigger as heroic for having killed her. Furthermore, he wants to emphasize that Bigger's mindset is one of such pain and rage that he is more than capable of committing such brutality. Bigger is a victim of racism, and the worst part of his victimization is not that he is forced to kill Mary but that he has been transformed into a person capable of furious violence, one who even craves such violence. Showing Bigger hacking apart Mary's corpse, Wright indelibly reminds us that Bigger is not morally pure. Rather, racism has destroyed Bigger's innocence by awakening terrible capabilities within him—capabilities that later enable him to kill Bessie as well.

3. "Listen, Bigger," said Britten. "Did you see this guy
    [Jan] act in any way out of the ordinary? I mean, sort
    of nervous, say? Just what *did* he talk about?"
        "He talked about Communists. . . ."
        "Did he ask you to join?"
        "He gave me that stuff to read."
        "Come on. Tell us some of the things he said."
        Bigger knew the things that white folks hated to
    hear Negroes ask for; and he knew that these were the
    things the Reds were always asking for.

In this passage from Book Two, in which Britten questions Bigger
about Mary's disappearance, we see Bigger's astute ability to deflect
suspicion away from himself by playing upon white prejudice
against blacks and communists. Bigger assumes a slow-witted, subservient attitude that completely conceals his sharp intellect and
capability for drastic action, and then uses this attitude to cast subtle suspicion upon the innocent Jan. Bigger utterly outsmarts the
whites by telling them exactly what they want to hear, saying that,
on the night of Mary's disappearance, Jan was talking about these
"things the Reds were always asking for." Bigger knows that simply
associating Jan with communist rhetoric will make Jan appear
guilty in the minds of his white listeners, even though they already
know Jan to be an avowed communist. Bigger uses his long experience with racial prejudice shrewdly, manipulating the prejudices of
his white questioners. This passage suggests that, had Mary's bones
not been discovered in the furnace, Bigger may have gotten away
with his crime completely.

QUOTATIONS

4. *He* had done this. *He* had brought all this about. In all
    of his life these two murders were the most
    meaningful things that had ever happened to him.

This quotation from Book Two is the first expression of an idea that
Max later echoes in his courtroom defense of Bigger—that Bigger's
murders make him as exultant as they make him guilty, as they provide his life with a new sense of purpose and expression. Bigger's
possibilities have always been stunted by racism, but after these
murderous acts, he is "free" to act—and to live with the consequences of these actions—for the first time. Even though these consequences ultimately mean flight and imprisonment, this feeling of
self-assertion and personal control nonetheless remains liberating
and intoxicating for Bigger.

5. There was something he *knew* and something he *felt*; something the *world* gave him and something he *himself* had. . . . [N]ever in all his life, with this black skin of his, had the two worlds, thought and feeling, will and mind, aspiration and satisfaction, been together; never had he felt a sense of wholeness.

Early on in *Native Son,* Wright describes how Bigger retreats behind a "wall" to keep the reality of his situation from overwhelming him. This passage from Book Two elucidates the destructive effects of Bigger's retreat. He is isolated not only from his friends and family, but from himself as well. The African-American author W. E. B. DuBois, in *The Souls of Black Folk,* describes the effect of racism on the black psyche: "One ever feels his two-ness—an American, a negro; two souls, two thoughts, two unreconciled strivings; two warring ideals in one dark body whose dogged strength alone keeps it from being torn asunder." Indeed, though Bigger's body is still in one piece, his mind is split in two, leaving him unable to interact with others and unable to understand himself. It is this quest for wholeness that dominates Bigger's life. Tragically, it is not until he has murdered two women and is soon to be executed that he is able to understand and grasp this wholeness. He is exhilarated by his new realization, yet tormented by the fact that it comes too late, when he has precious little time left to live.

QUOTATIONS

KEY FACTS

FULL TITLE
Native Son

AUTHOR
Richard Wright

TYPE OF WORK
Novel

GENRE
Urban naturalism; novel of social protest

LANGUAGE
English

TIME AND PLACE WRITTEN
1938–1939, Brooklyn, New York

DATE OF FIRST PUBLICATION
1940

PUBLISHER
Harper and Brothers

NARRATOR
The story is narrated in a limited third-person voice that focuses on Bigger Thomas's thoughts and feelings.

POINT OF VIEW
The story is told almost exclusively from Bigger's perspective.

TONE
The narrator's attitude toward his subject is one of absorption. The narrator is preoccupied with bringing us into Bigger's mind and situation, using short, evocative sentences to tell the story. Though the narrator is clearly opposed to the destructive racism that the novel chronicles, there is very little narrative editorializing, though some characters, such as Max, make statements that evoke a secondary tone of social protest in the final part of the novel.

TENSE
Past

SETTING (TIME)
1930s

SETTING (PLACE)
Chicago

PROTAGONIST
Bigger Thomas

MAJOR CONFLICT
The fear, hatred, and anger that racism has impressed upon Bigger Thomas ravages his individuality so severely that his only means of self-expression is violence. After killing Mary Dalton, Bigger must contend with the law, the hatred of society, and his own destructive inner feelings.

RISING ACTION
The planned robbery of Blum's deli; Bigger's trip to the movies; Bigger's night with Mary and Jan

CLIMAX
Each of the three books of the novel has its own climax: Book One climaxes with the murder of Mary, Book Two with the discovery of Mary's remains in the furnace, and Book Three with the culmination of Bigger's trial in the death sentence.

FALLING ACTION
Bigger's trial and his relationship with Boris A. Max

THEMES
The effect of racism on the oppressed; the effect of racism on the oppressor; the hypocrisy of justice

MOTIFS
Popular culture; religion; communism

SYMBOLS
Mrs. Dalton's blindness; the cross; snow

FORESHADOWING
Buckley's campaign poster; Bigger's occasional premonitions that he will do something violent and impulsive

KEY FACTS

STUDY QUESTIONS & ESSAY TOPICS

STUDY QUESTIONS

1. In what ways does Wright portray Bigger's day-to-day existence as a prison, even before his arrest and trial?

The crowded, rat-infested apartment Bigger shares with his brother, sister, and mother is, in a sense, a prison cell. Bigger is imprisoned in the urban ghetto by racist rental policies. Likewise, his own consciousness is a prison, as a sense of failure, inadequacy, and unrelenting fear pervades his entire life. Racist white society, Bigger's mother, and even Bigger himself all believe that he is destined to meet a bad end. Bigger's relentless conviction that he faces an inevitably disastrous fate indicates his feeling that he has absolutely no control over his life. Society permits him access only to menial jobs, poor housing, and little or no opportunity for education—on the whole, he has no choice but a substandard life.

2.   *Describe the real estate practices that were applied to*
      black families in Chicago's South Side in the 1930s. With
      these practices in mind, why is Mr. Dalton—an avowed
      philanthropist toward blacks—a hypocrite?

Although ample housing was available in most sections of 1930s Chicago, white property owners imposed agreements that enabled blacks to rent apartments only on the city's South Side. These limitations created an artificial housing shortage, allowing landlords to increase rents on the South Side despite the deplorable conditions of many of their buildings. Mr. Dalton has earned much of his fortune from such racist rental policies, which he considers customary and does not even think to consider unethical. In this manner, Mr. Dalton contributes significantly toward the social disparities that terrify, oppress, and enrage blacks such as Bigger. Given his actions, Mr. Dalton's charitable donations to the black community are merely meaningless tokens—condescending and patronizing gestures. Mr. Dalton expresses his so-called benevolence by giving Bigger a menial job, but, as Max says, Dalton does so only in an attempt to erase the guilt he feels for his role in oppressing blacks in the first place.

3. *Describe Jan and Mary's attitude toward race relations. In what ways does their more subtle racism resemble the more overt prejudice of other whites?*

To Jan and Mary, breaking social taboos is a thrill. They derive an odd satisfaction from eating in a black restaurant with Bigger. They clearly want to experience "blackness," yet come nowhere near an understanding of the frustration and hopelessness that constitutes blackness for Bigger. Mary and Jan are, in effect, merely entertaining themselves by slumming in the ghetto with Bigger. Like the Daltons, then, they are blind to the social reality of blackness. Moreover, Mary uses the same language that racists such as Peggy use to describe black Americans. When talking to Bigger, Mary uses the phrase "your people" and refers to black Americans as "they" and "them." Her language implies that there is an alien, foreign aura to black Americans, that they are somehow a separate, essentially different class of human beings. Mary's remark about "our country" is also telling, as it indicates that she assigns ownership of America to white people in her mind. In the act of claiming that "[t]hey're human," Mary still maintains a psychological division between white and black Americans. Although she briefly seems to recognize Bigger's feelings, she still has not reached the point at which she can say, "*We're* human."

4.   *How does Bigger's desperate flight from the police*
     symbolize his existence as a whole?

The manhunt, which is conducted entirely by whites, literally corrals Bigger in an shrinking cross-section of Chicago. "Whiteness"
pursues Bigger through an intense building-by-building search of
the entire South Side. Like a cornered rat, Bigger desperately moves
within this ever shrinking square, trying to evade the "whiteness"
that has, in a sense, cornered and corralled him his entire life. This
"whiteness" has always pursued Bigger, policed him, and stood
ready to punish him if he crosses the "line." The snowstorm that
rages during the manhunt is a literal symbol of this metaphorical
"whiteness," surrounding and crippling Bigger by preventing him
from leaving the city. Like the waves of white men searching for
him, the snow falls relentlessly around Bigger, locking him in place.
Literally and symbolically, "whiteness" falls on Bigger's head with
the power of a natural disaster.

5. *As Wright portrays it, how does the psychology of racial prejudice contribute to Bigger's transformation into a murderer and a criminal?*

In killing a white woman, Bigger does what the white American majority has always feared he might do. The whites are convinced that he raped Mary first—a violation of the ultimate social taboo that separates black men from white women. In an effort to keep Bigger from doing what they have feared, the empowered majority of whites have narrowed the boundaries of his existence and kept him in constant fear. Instead of ensuring his submission, however, this confinement has caused Bigger to respond to his overwhelming fear of "whiteness" by doing exactly what the empowered majority always feared he would do. In response to his crime, the white-dominated press and authorities incite mob hatred against him. They portray Bigger as bestial, inhuman rapist and killer of white women. This viciously racist portrayal of Bigger—and the white mob fury it engenders—gives the whites a justification to terrorize all of the South Side in an attempt to frighten the entire black community. In this chain of events, Wright depicts the irrational logic of racism, effectively a vicious cycle that reproduces itself over and over again.

6.   *Is Bigger's trial a fair one? In Wright's portrayal, how does racism affect the American judicial process? What role does the media play in determining popular conceptions of justice?*

Bigger's trial is unfair from the start, and it is clear that the proceedings are merely a spectacle. Bigger's guilt and punishment are decided before his trial ever begins, perhaps even before he is arrested. The newspapers do not refer to him as the suspect or the accused, but rather as the "Negro Rapist Murderer." There is no question that Bigger will be sentenced to death. Nonetheless, the public still feels the need to go through the motions of justice. The public may desire to build a wall of hysteria surrounding Bigger in order to justify its racist stereotypes, yet it also attempts to deny its racism by creating the illusion of equal treatment under the law. As Max argues later, there is a component of guilt in this hateful hysteria, as it represents an attempt on the part of the empowered majority to deny its responsibility in Bigger's crimes. The illusion of equality under the law disguises the economic inequality that has condemned Bigger to a hopeless, impoverished urban ghetto and a series of menial low-wage jobs. Edward Robertson, an editor of the *Jackson Daily Star,* states that keeping the black population in constant fear ensures its submission. However, as Bigger's life demonstrates, this constant fear actually causes violence. In this sense, the empowered majority sows the seeds of minority violence in the very act of trying to quell it.

Suggested Essay Topics

1. Describe the psychological and behavioral change that overcomes Bigger during the interview with Mr. Dalton. Why does he change in the presence of Mr. Dalton? In what way is it significant that Bigger goes to the movies before going to the Daltons'?

2. What are some of the real historical events that occur or are mirrored in *Native Son*? How does Wright weave these events into his fictional narrative, and how does this technique affect the novel as a whole?

3. What role does imagery of vision and sight play in *Native Son*? Think especially of Mrs. Dalton's blindness and Bigger's murder of Mary.

4. How does popular culture serve as a form of indoctrination throughout *Native Son*?

Review & Resources

Quiz

1. Why does Bigger attack Gus when they meet up to rob Blum's delicatessen?

    A. Gus does not want to rob Blum's delicatessen anymore
    B. Gus insults Bigger
    C. Bigger wants to sabotage the robbery
    D. Gus has forgotten to bring his gun

2. Why does Bigger hate his family?

    A. They refuse to work and he has to support them
    B. They threaten to turn him in to the police
    C. They criticize his friends
    D. They are miserable and he is unable to help them

3. Who hires Bigger as a chauffeur?

    A. Mr. Dalton
    B. Buckley
    C. Boris A. Max
    D. Jan Erlone

4. Why does Bigger kill Mary?

    A. She attacks him
    B. He is terrified of being found alone in her bedroom with her
    C. He wants to steal the money in her purse
    D. He wants to collect ransom from her parents

5. Who is Mr. Dalton?

    A. The State's Attorney
    B. A politician
    C. A doctor
    D. A real estate baron

6. Why does Bigger kill Bessie?

    A. He knows that her complaining and her alcoholism
        will slow him down in his flight from the police
    B. He does not want her to turn him in to the police for
        raping her
    C. She has spent some of his money
    D. She threatens to turn him in for killing Mary

7. Why do Mary's parents disapprove of her relationship
    with Jan?

    A. Jan does not come from a wealthy background
    B. Jan gets Mary drunk too often
    C. Jan is a communist
    D. Jan believes in racial equality

8. Who is Britten?

    A. A policeman
    B. A private investigator
    C. A reporter
    D. Mary's uncle

9. From what handicap does Mrs. Dalton suffer?

    A. Blindness
    B. Paralysis
    C. Deafness
    D. Muteness

10. Which of the following describes Max?

    A. He is an attorney for the Labor Defenders
    B. He is Jewish
    C. He is Bigger's lawyer
    D. All of the above

11. Who is Buckley?

    A. A policeman
    B. The judge who presides over Bigger's trial
    C. A private investigator
    D. The State's Attorney

12. How does Bigger react to Mary's unreserved behavior toward him?

    A.   He is angry
    B.   He is afraid
    C.   He is ashamed
    D.   All of the above

13. Why is Bigger alone with Mary in her bedroom the night he kills her?

    A.   He has to help her to her bedroom, as she is too drunk to get up the stairs herself
    B.   He wants to get her drunk so he will not have to take her to the station in the morning
    C.   She wants to read some communist pamphlets with him
    D.   She wants him to help her pack for her trip to Detroit in the morning

14. Why does Buckley rush Bigger's trial?

    A.   Bigger has already confessed to his crimes, so the trial is irrelevant at this point
    B.   He is afraid a riot will break out if he does not conclude the trial quickly
    C.   The case against Bigger is so strong that the outcome is inevitable
    D.   The trial will give him a political advantage in his upcoming campaign for reelection

15. How does Bigger's mother cope with her misery?

    A.   She drinks
    B.   She is devoutly religious
    C.   She abuses her children
    D.   She goes to the movies

16. What is the first violent act Bigger commits during the novel?

    A.   He attacks Gus without provocation or warning
    B.   He robs Blum's delicatessen at gunpoint
    C.   He kills a rat in his family's apartment
    D.   He kills Mary Dalton

17. What does Buddy think about Bigger's job with the Daltons?

     A.   Buddy envies Bigger's job
     B.   Buddy thinks Bigger's job is degrading and menial
     C.   Buddy thinks Bigger's job is boring
     D.   Buddy does not think Bigger's job pays enough

18. What does Bigger do with Mary's body?

     A.   He hides it in Mary's trunk
     B.   He throws it down an airshaft in an empty building
          on the South Side
     C.   He buries it
     D.   He burns it in the Daltons' furnace

19. Where does Bigger first see Mary Dalton?

     A.   At his job interview
     B.   In a newsreel at a movie theater
     C.   At Ernie's Kitchen Shack on the South Side
     D.   At Blum's delicatessen

20. Why does Bigger *not* flee Chicago after Mary's bones
     are discovered?

     A.   The police block every road in and out of the city
     B.   He decides it is better just to give up
     C.   A snowstorm blocks all roads in and out of the city
     D.   Bigger does not want to leave his family

21. What happened to Bigger's father?

     A.   He abandoned the family when Bigger was ten years old
     B.   He was killed in a riot in the South
     C.   He was arrested, convicted, and executed for murder
     D.   He committed suicide

22. What famous court cases parallel Bigger's trial?

   A. The Lindbergh kidnapping and murder case
   B. The Scopes trial and the Brown v. Board of
      Education case
   C. The Dred Scott case and the Loeb-Leopold
      kidnapping and murder trial
   D. The Nixon case and the Loeb-Leopold kidnapping
      and murder trial

23. To which literary genre does *Native Son* belong?

   A. Urban naturalism
   B. Romanticism
   C. Transcendentalism
   D. All of the above

24. Why are rents on the South Side higher than in other
    Chicago neighborhoods?

   A. It is an upscale neighborhood with nice apartments
   B. The rents on the South Side include all utility bills
   C. The rents are not higher on the South Side than in
      other neighborhoods
   D. Racist rental policies have created an artificial housing
      shortage on the South Side

25. Who is the author of *Native Son*?

   A. James Baldwin
   B. Richard Wright
   C. Ralph Ellison
   D. Langston Hughes

Answer Key:
1: C; 2: D; 3: A; 4: B; 5: D; 6: A; 7: C; 8: B; 9: A; 10: D; 11:
D; 12: D; 13: A; 14: D; 15: B; 16: C; 17: A; 18: D; 19: B; 20:
C; 21: B; 22: D; 23: A; 24: D; 25: B

Suggestions for Further Reading

ALGEO, ANN. *The Courtroom as Forum: Homicide Trials by Dreiser, Wright, Capote, and Mailer.* New York: Peter Lang, 1996.

BEAUVAIS, PAUL JUDE. *Richard Wright's* NATIVE SON. New York: Chelsea House, 1988.

BRIGNANO, RUSSELL C. *Richard Wright: An Introduction to the Man and His Works.* Pittsburgh: University of Pittsburgh Press, 1970.

DUBOIS, W. E. B. *The Souls of Black Folk.* New York: Bantam Books, 1989.

FELGAR, ROBERT. *Richard Wright.* Boston: Twayne Publishers, 1980.

GATES, HENRY LOUIS, JR., and K. A. APPIAH, eds. *Richard Wright: Critical Perspectives Past and Present.* New York: Amistad Press, 1993.

KINNAMON, KENNETH, ed. *Critical Essays on Richard Wright's* NATIVE SON. Boston: Twayne Publishers, 1997.

MILLER, EUGENE E. *Voice of a Native Son: The Poetics of Richard Wright.* Jackson: University Press of Mississippi, 1990.

WRIGHT, RICHARD. *Black Boy.* New York: HarperCollins, 1998.

REVIEW & RESOURCES

SparkNotes Study Guides: